AF594386

Living Histories

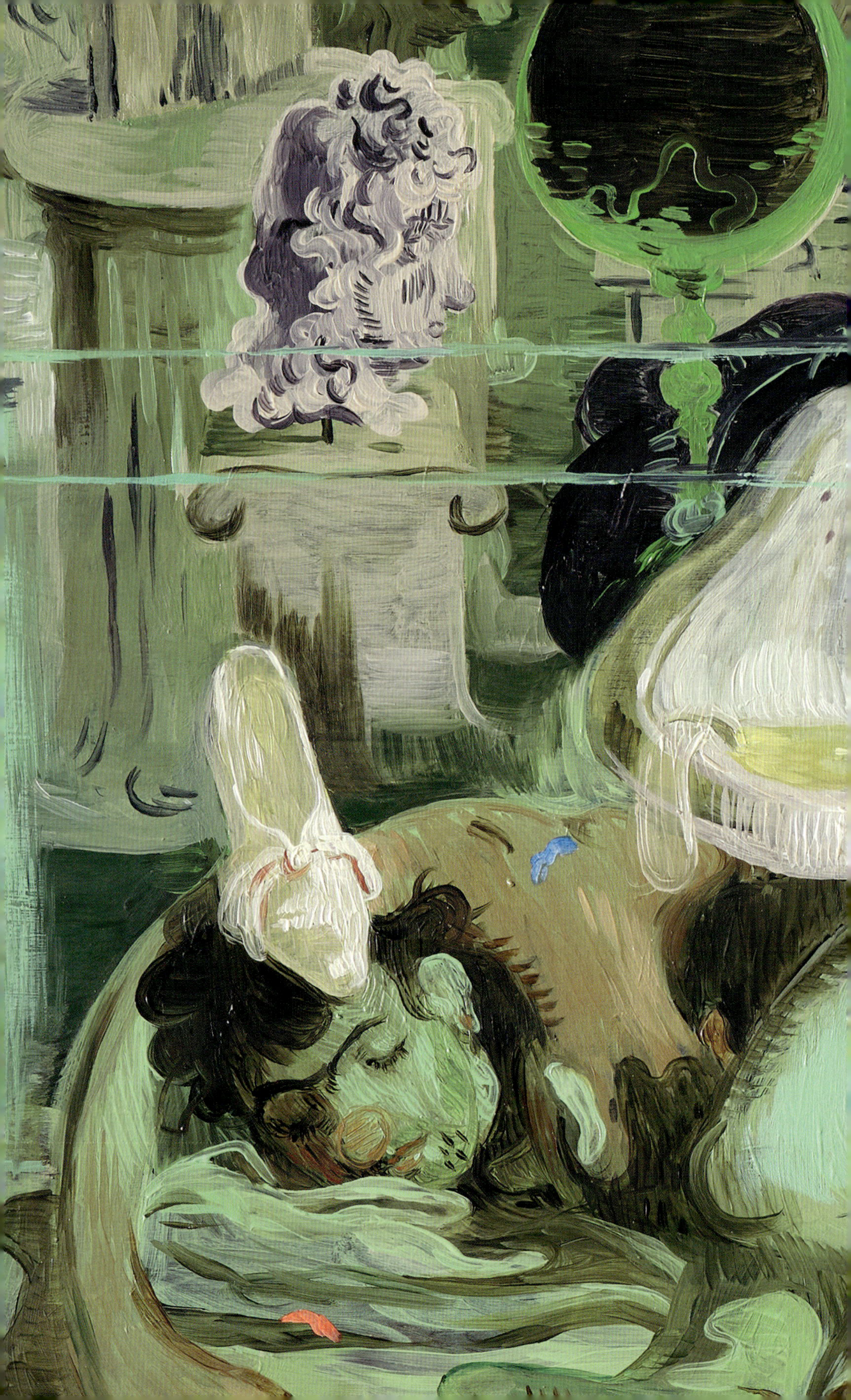

LIVING HISTORIES

Queer Views and Old Masters

Aimee Ng, Xavier F. Salomon, and Stephen Truax

Foreword by Hanya Yanagihara

With contributions by Jonathan Anderson, Jessica Bell Brown, Jenna Gribbon, Doron Langberg, Christopher Y. Lew, Toyin Ojih Odutola, Jason Reynolds, Legacy Russell, Salman Toor, and Russell Tovey

g

The Frick Collection, New York in association with D Giles Limited

This publication is generously funded by
Dr. Tai-Heng Cheng and Cole Harrell.

First published in 2023 by The Frick Collection
1 East 70th Street
New York, NY 10021
www.frick.org

Michaelyn Mitchell, Editor in Chief
Christopher Snow Hopkins, Associate Editor

In association with GILES
An imprint of D Giles Limited
66 High Street
Lewes, BN7 1XG, UK
gilesltd.com

Copyedited and proofread by Sarah Kane
Designed by Alfonso Iacurci
Produced by GILES
Printed and bound in Italy

Front cover: Doron Langberg, *Lover* (detail), 2021 (cat. 2)
Back cover: Hans Holbein the Younger, *Sir Thomas More* (detail), 1527 (fig. 16)
Frontispiece: Salman Toor, *Museum Boys* (detail), 2021 (cat. 3)
p. 4: fig. 31
p. 12: fig. 24
pp. 6, 14, 20, 30, 36, 48, 58, 70, 84, 100: details of cat. nos. 1–4
p. 44: fig. 16

A CIP catalogue record for this book is available from the Library of Congress.
ISBN: 978-1-913875-39-8

FSC
www.fsc.org
MIX
Paper | Supporting responsible forestry
FSC® C021437

Contents

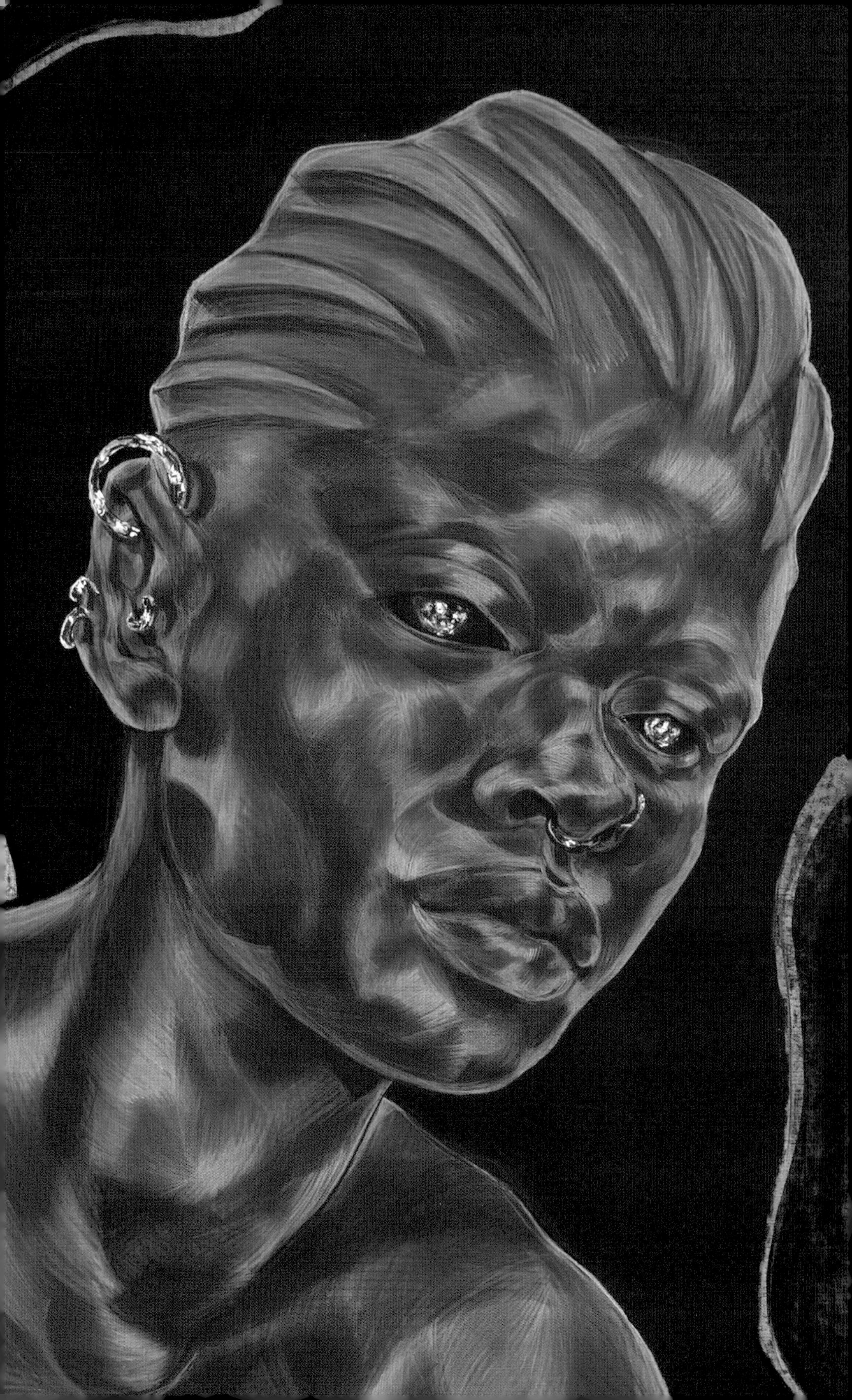

Foreword

Look at Us

Hanya Yanagihara

The art of portraiture is as old as art itself; indeed, it is almost as old as humanity. As soon as humans figured out how to render pictures, mixing earth and fat and bits of burnt wood and bone, they were creating images of the life they saw around them.

And that meant creating, significantly, images of other people. Portraiture was a way to celebrate, as well as to commemorate: a human dies, but his face endures. The creation of a portrait was, and remains, among the most intimate of artistic acts, as it involves one person conjuring somebody else's visage. From one hand, the face of another.

It is why, perhaps, some of the most memorable works of Western art are portraits: Mona Lisa, the girl with her luminous pearl earring, Infanta Margarita Teresa in a dress as wide as a house. These are works that feel almost elemental to us. We cannot remember where or when we first encountered them, but it's as if we've known them all along. What keeps us looking, again and again, are the sitters' expressions, just beyond the reach of our understanding.

So it makes sense that the first thing we usually want to know about a portrait is not "Who painted that?" but "Who is she?" More often than not, the answer—someone rich, someone grand, someone significant, someone beautiful—is why, arguably, portrait painting fell so dramatically out of fashion in the modern era. What room was there in the twentieth century, with its new technologies and new recognition of divisions and injustices, for more celebrations of people with money or birthright? What time was there in the machine age to sit for hours for an artist with a brush? The world has always been made by the common person, but art history has not and portrait painting least of all.

It's also why the past decade or so has seen a renaissance of figurative painting, especially portraiture. Who gets to be considered a worthy subject? Whose image gets to hang on the wall of a museum? Who, in other words, do we think is important? The reply—*we* are—has come from all kinds of artists who, by virtue of their race or gender or sexuality or education, have been rarely seen in museums. The return of portraiture—specifically, portrait paintings, a medium that demands commitment from both the artist and the sitter—is a correction and a progression, a recalibrating of not only who we look at, but who does the looking.

~

That's why there's something mischievously subversive about *Living Histories*. Like painting, gayness too is as old as humanity; yet for millennia, we saw it recorded or depicted mostly in glimpses, in code. For most of history, gay people, as well as anyone outside of heteronormativity, spent their lives as sleuths, always on the lookout for evidence of themselves: that they existed; that someone else recognized that existence.

By inviting four of the most exciting and inventive young artists working today to make paintings for the Frick, the curators—Xavier F. Salomon and Aimee Ng—create something genuinely disruptive, in the true sense of the word. To walk into those galleries, so familiar in their stateliness, their sober beauty, and encounter at their heart Salman Toor's woozy, vivid, unsettling tribute to Western art; Doron Langberg's tender yet ecstatic vision of a shirtless man; Jenna Gribbon's confident, unflinching rendering of her confident, unflinching partner; and Toyin Ojih Odutola's convincing and compelling imagined warrior is to be forced to reckon with all our old, half-buried ideas about what art, and which people, matter. The fact that they are placed in conversation with some of the museum's best known and most celebrated works—Johannes Vermeer's *Officer and Laughing Girl* (ca. 1657) and *Mistress and Maid* (1666–67); Hans Holbein the Younger's *Sir Thomas More* (1527); Holbein's *Thomas Cromwell* (1532–33); and Rembrandt's *Self-Portrait* (1658) and *Nicolaes Ruts* (1631), respectively—is not a defensive act but a generous one. It invites us to see anew pictures that the eye has seen so often that it can (shamefully) glance over them. The pieces lend one another dignity, but fresh relevance as well.

On the Saturdays I visited the museum, first for Langberg's and Toor's works, then for Gribbon's and Odutola's, I found myself drawn back to their portraits (and their companions) again and again. What was it, I wondered, that I found so moving about these juxtapositions, both so unexpected but also—upon looking at them closely—so inevitable?

In the end, I decided that it was not how little the four commissioned painters shared with their predecessors; it was how much. The newcomers had no right to be in the Frick. They're gay. Two of them are women. Only one was born in the West. They're alive. Yet they had *every* right—they're painters, after all. Their studios, and practices, and lives, and loves might look far different from those of their artistic ancestors. But I think those long-gone artists would have recognized something of themselves in their heirs' understanding of color, in their patience, in their need to see, and to speak. They would have understood that these interlopers were doing the same work they had. And when they did, they would have moved over and made some room for them on the walls. *Look at me*, a portrait says, *I am here. Someone witnessed me; I witnessed them back*. All we have to do is obey.

Director's Preface

The move to Frick Madison has been liberating. Displaying magnificent works of art in sumptuous buildings of 1914 and 1935 is the essence of The Frick Collection's appeal and will continue to seduce visitors once the art returns to its renovated quarters. Yet our temporary residence five blocks north of the permanent site has prompted an extraordinary opportunity. The mansion's domestic character—a Spanish painting over a mantelpiece in the Living Hall, for example, or a porcelain garniture on a French commode in the Dining Room—reflects the personality of Henry Clay Frick. By contrast, Marcel Breuer's 1966 building, while forceful architecture, was designed to be neutral to accommodate rotating exhibitions. These spaces inspired the re-envisioning of our collection that has captivated so many visitors.

A series of galleries on three floors, Frick Madison has been tailored to our collection yet is simple to change and to reinstall. The building's adaptability, coupled with the unique opportunity to lend some of our paintings during renovation, has been a seedbed for a series of projects pairing contemporary with older art. The first of these was *Living Histories: Queer Views and Old Masters*. It was followed by a painting by Olafur Eliasson placed next to one by Claude Monet in the context of the Frick Diptych book series. An installation by Nicolas Party and an exhibition on Barkley L. Hendricks will follow. As the loans of our paintings to other museums left gaps on our walls, we invited Salman Toor, Doron Langberg, Jenna Gribbon, and Toyin Ojih Odutola—named in the order of the installations, which took place over a year—to make a work in response to the missing painting and to those that remained. The surprise of seeing art of our time in the company of the work of previous centuries at the Frick sparks a dialogue. The three paintings and one drawing that the artists created raised a host of questions about the role of sexual identity in portraiture, about the strategies a painter uses to convey an individual's character, about the very nature of representing a sitter today. We are grateful to the artists for participating in this project, for their lively contributions to panel discussions and video interviews, and for their part in making this book.

We also thank their gallerists, who facilitated the process of commissioning and bringing the works here. Hanya Yanagihara kindly agreed to write a foreword, and we are delighted with her eloquent text. We thank the contributors and Stephen Truax, who coedited the book with Xavier F. Salomon, Deputy Director and Peter Jay Sharp Chief Curator, and Aimee Ng, Curator. As director, I am fortunate to work alongside such talented and creative curators as Xavier and Aimee. This project was their idea, and their essays articulate the meaning and resonance of the whole undertaking. Finally, I owe deep appreciation to our trustee Tai-Heng Cheng and his husband Cole Harrell for providing funding for this book, one of many initiatives they have supported to further diversity at the Frick.

Ian Wardropper
Anna-Maria and Stephen Kellen Director
The Frick Collection

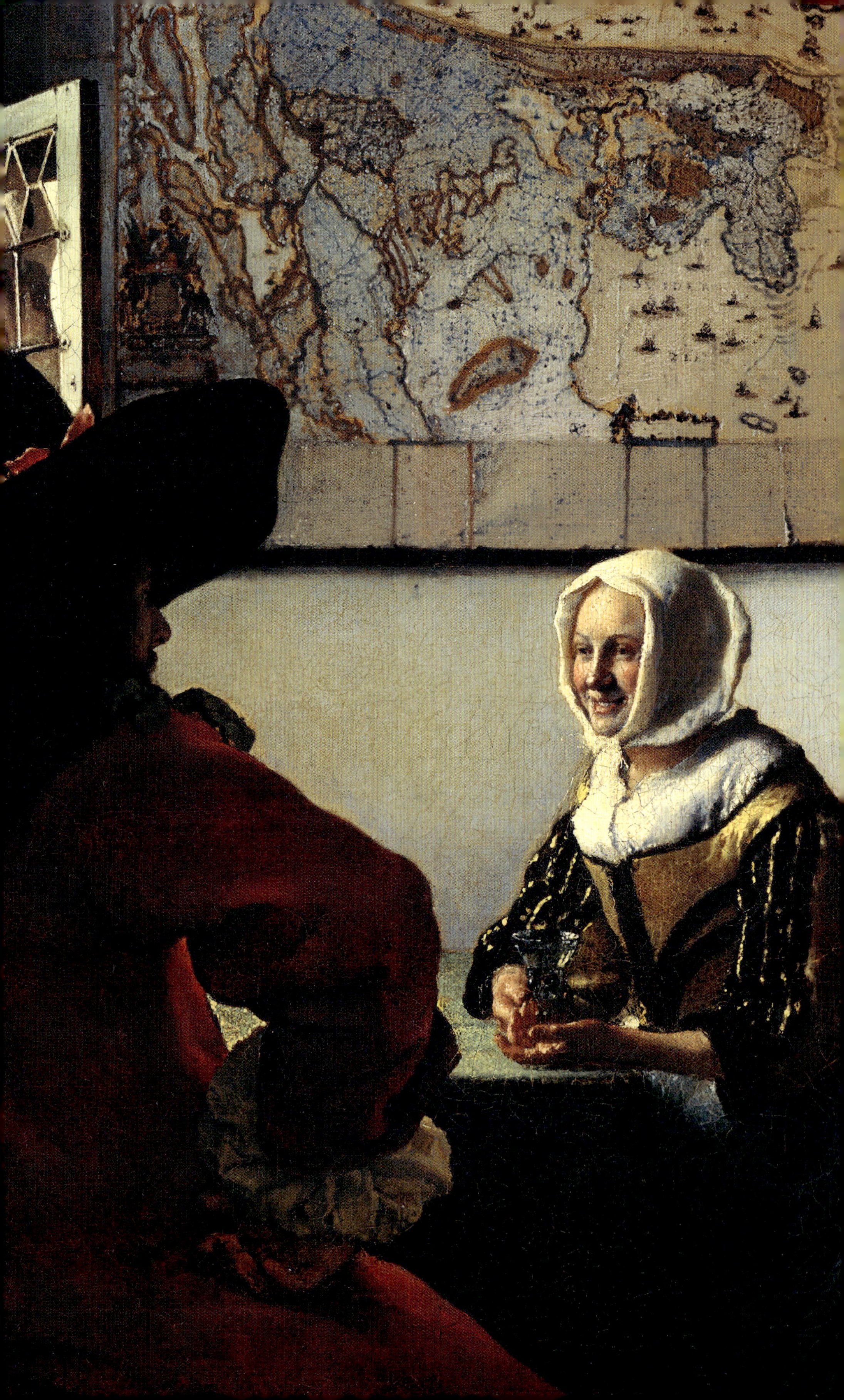

Acknowledgments

This project is the result of collaborations and conversations with friends and colleagues from around the world, which have been profoundly meaningful and insightful and for which we are deeply grateful. First and foremost, our thanks go to Ian Wardropper, the Anna-Maria and Stephen Kellen Director of the Frick, for his steadfast support of a project that is so unlike anything else in the museum's history. Together with Ian, Betty Eveillard, chair of the Frick's Board of Trustees, gave us judicious counsel and support. We thank the Frick's Editor in Chief, Michaelyn Mitchell, who helped shape this publication and marshal its production while expertly editing its many components. We are also grateful to the Frick's Associate Editor, Christopher Snow Hopkins, for his significant editorial contributions. Curatorial Assistants Rebecca Leonard and Gemma McElroy worked tirelessly alongside us at every stage of the year-long project of *Living Histories* and its subsequent publication, and we owe them our deepest thanks. Also at the Frick, we are grateful to Anna Baccaglini, Joseph Coscia Jr., Giulio Dalvit, Arthur Fowler, Allison Galea, Lisa Goble, Joseph Godla, Caitlin Henningsen, Patrick King, George Koelle, Alexis Light, Christopher Roberson, Heidi Rosenau, April Kim Tonin, and Sean Troxell. We are always grateful to exhibition designer Stephen Saitas and to lighting designer Anita Jorgensen and her team.

The galleries that represent the four artists involved in the *Living Histories* project have been generous collaborators. We thank the teams at Fredericks & Freiser and MASSIMODECARLO; Victoria Miro, especially Will Davies, Jessica Green, and Glenn Scott Wright; Jack Shainman Gallery, especially Joeonna Bellorado-Samuels and Lydia Cardenas; and Luhring Augustine, especially Caroline Burghardt, Nancy Ford, Sasha Helinski, and Donald Johnson-Montenegro. We would also like to thank Esther Adler, Horace Ballard, Ilan Cohen, Kyle Coniglio, Roxane Gay, Thomas McCarty, Michał Przygoda, Antwaun Sargent, Mackenzie Scott, Ali Sethi, and Andrew Smith.

We have been honored by the participation of catalogue contributors Jonathan Anderson, Jessica Bell Brown, Christopher Y. Lew, Jason Reynolds, Legacy Russell, Russell Tovey, and Hanya Yanagihara. They bring to this project the riches of their work in a variety of cultural fields, and we are very grateful to them for engaging in *Living Histories* so wholeheartedly.

Above all, we offer our thanks to the artists. Jenna Gribbon, Doron Langberg, Toyin Ojih Odutola, and Salman Toor shared their art and much more with us and with the Frick's audiences. Their insights, talents, and inspiration have allowed us to see long-familiar works in the Frick's collection in new ways.

Aimee Ng, Xavier F. Salomon, and Stephen Truax

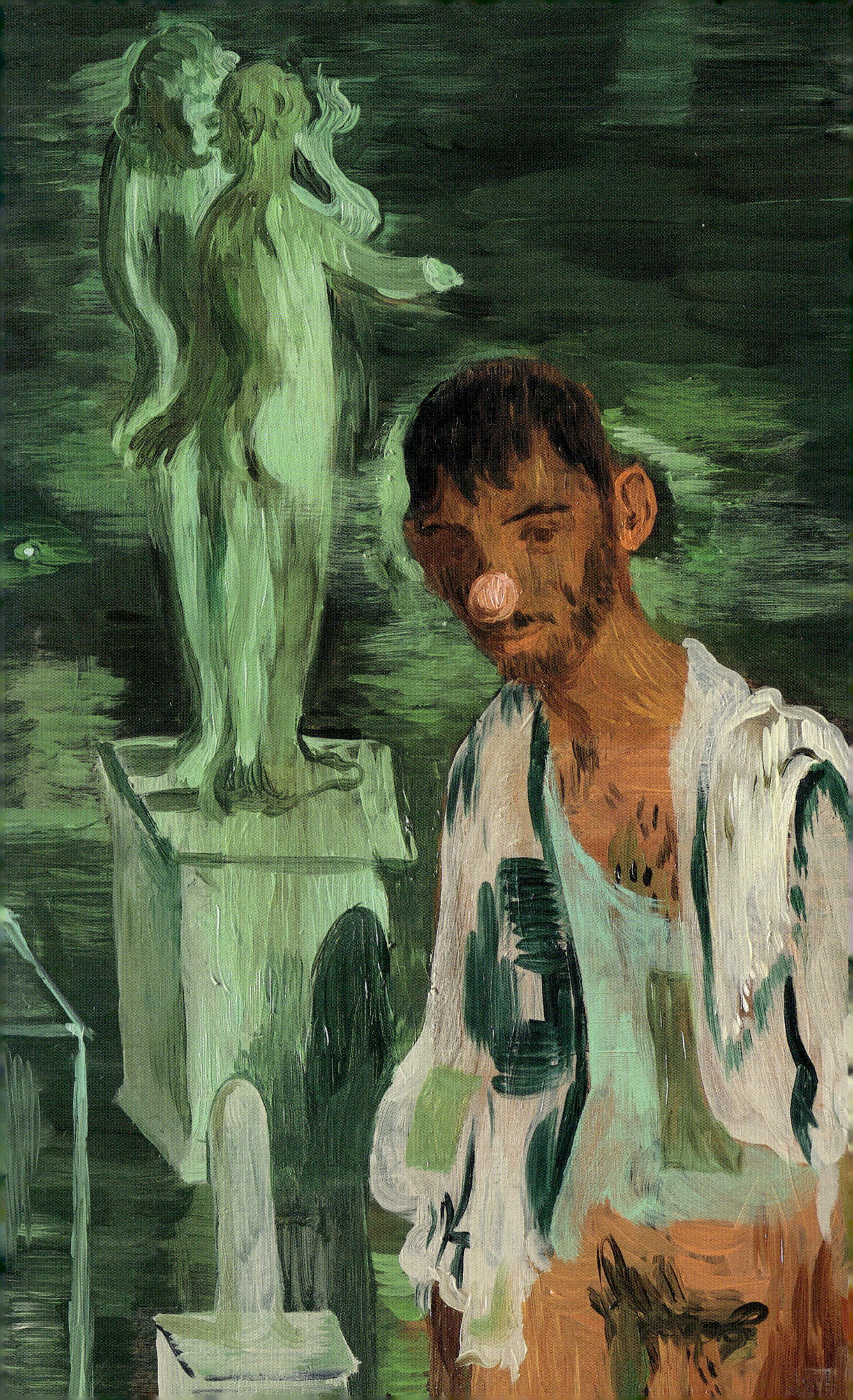

Introduction

Why

Xavier F. Salomon

Let's go down to the water's edge
And we can cast away those doubts
Some things are better left unsaid
But they still turn me inside out
—Annie Lennox, 1992

The industrialist Henry Clay Frick was an avid collector of painted portraits. He particularly relished bringing together pendants that, through the vagaries of history, had found their way to different collections. In 1905, the year he moved to New York, Frick purchased a portrait of Margaret Helen Gerard (Mrs. James Cruikshank) by the Scottish painter Henry Raeburn. The work had been painted around 1805–9 for her husband, as a pendant to his own portrait. In 1899, the paintings were separated when the grandson of the couple sold them. In 1911, six years after Frick purchased the picture of Margaret, he acquired the one of her husband. Two other portraits united by Frick are those of Frans Snyders and his wife, Margareta de Vos, painted by Anthony van Dyck around 1620. Frick purchased them in 1909—Frans from Castle Howard and Margareta from Warwick Castle. They had been separated since 1793. In 1910, he purchased *Portrait of a Man* by Frans Hals, thinking he was reuniting it with Hals's *Portrait of a Woman*, which at the time was believed to be its pendant. However, it later transpired that they were unrelated.

One striking feature of the portraits at the Frick is that whenever they were created as pendants, they invariably represent a husband and wife. In 1912, Frick purchased the iconic painting of Sir Thomas More by Hans Holbein the Younger, one of the museum's masterpieces. It could not be paired with a portrait of his wife, Lady Alice More, as a pendant seems never to have been painted. Instead, Frick paired the portrait of More with one of his enemy, Thomas Cromwell, a painting he bought in 1915. The two sitters have glared at each other across the chimneypiece of the Frick's Living Hall for more than a century now, two men reunited in everlasting hatred. This, however, is the only instance of paintings of two men displayed as pendants at the Frick. At a time in history when the concept of marriage has drastically shifted, how can The Frick Collection—with all its art created in countries and at times when homosexuality was a punishable offense—represent today's Queer community? An area not represented at the Frick—mostly due to the social, political, and religious history of Europe—relates to the love (or sexual) lives of the artists represented in the collection. Many of them were married, some were not. Some of them may have been primarily interested in those of their own sex—Agnolo Bronzino comes to mind. Of course, in sixteenth-century Florence, identifying as a "sodomite" would have led to a death sentence or, at best, a fine and time in prison.

The museum Frick created for his collection is dedicated to European art between the thirteenth century and 1900. As such, it is by no means encyclopedic; even within its scope, there are gaps. The Frick has no holdings of seventeenth-century Italian paintings (and very few religious paintings in general); no Spanish sculpture; no Dutch, Flemish, or German furniture; no British decorative art; no Scandinavian painting. The list goes on. By the standards of European art and in the time frame covered by the Frick, the absences by far outweigh the presences. Even though non-white subjects are occasionally found in European art, none of these depictions are at the Frick—let alone any works by non-white artists, a rarity in European art. Women artists, by virtue of their place in society during the six hundred years covered by the Frick, are virtually invisible. In 1916, Frick acquired a pair of saltcellars with scenes from the story of Orpheus by Suzanne de Court. A businesswoman and extraordinary artist in sixteenth-century France, De Court managed the only enamel workshop in Limoges run by a woman. Frick, however, did not buy the two pieces for this reason. He bought them because they came as part of a larger group of enamel objects that had belonged to J. P. Morgan and that he purchased en bloc. The few works by women artists at the Frick came into the collection long after Frick's death and mostly in recent years: a portrait by Césarine-Henriette-Flore Davin-Mirvault (bought in 1952, when it was believed to be by Davin-Mirvault's teacher, Jacques-Louis David), two pastels by Rosalba Carriera (bequeathed to the museum in 2020), and another pastel by Elisabeth-Louise Vigée Le Brun (a promised gift to the museum). Many other groups of artists, sitters, and patrons are not represented at the Frick. In the future, the institution may be able to fill some of these gaps; some can only be resolved through exhibitions and programming.

Not until the nineteenth century was homosexuality discussed as it is now, and the word *homosexuality* is fraught even today, for both those who identify as such and those who do not. The word *queer*, used in the late nineteenth century with a pejorative meaning, has been reclaimed since the 1980s by many people in and outside the community; now it broadly describes anyone not complying with conventional heteronormative expectations. In a wide community, describing an infinite spectrum of feelings, emotions, and desires, the term *queer* has been used by a number of people under the umbrella, created in the 1990s, of the LGBT (lesbian, gay, bisexual, transgender) community, which has since expanded to LGBTQIA+ (adding to the list intersex and asexual with a plus denoting any other parts of the community not precisely described by the previous words).

In 1919, when Frick died, sodomy was illegal in the United States. It started to become legal in some states in the 1960s, but across the nation, only in 2003. What happened in the Queer community in the United States, and especially in New York, in the century that stretches from 1919 to 2021 cannot be adequately summarized here, but it includes fundamental (and traumatic) steps, starting with Gay Liberation in the 1960s, the Stonewall riots in 1969, and the AIDS epidemic of the 1980s. Same-sex marriage was finally legalized in the United States in 2015. The victories of the Queer community have been a major part of the progress of the United States. However, it cannot be forgotten that at least sixty-nine countries still criminalize homosexuality, the punishment ranging from years in prison, to whipping, hard labor, and death (stoning usually being the preferred method). And even in countries where homosexuality is legal—the United States among them—the condemnation of the Queer community is hardly a rare occurrence.

~

In the summer of 2018, I saw *Intimacy*, an exhibition curated by Stephen Truax at Yossi Milo Gallery. Included were paintings, photography, sculpture, and works on paper dating from the 1970s through the present and tracing the representation of intimate moments in the Queer community. The show featured works by pioneering Queer artists such as Paul Cadmus, Patrick Angus, Hugh Steers, and David Wojnarowicz. I was struck by how in the 1970s and '80s—especially at the height of the AIDS crisis—Queer artists found their voice most powerfully through photography. Along with examples of works by George Dureau, Robert Mapplethorpe, and Peter Hujar, the show included a new generation—one my age or younger that I could identify with—that had chosen figurative painting as a powerful instrument to portray Queer intimacy and relationships. The foundations of their work, as Truax posited, were based on the work of painters such as Cadmus, Angus, Steers, and David Hockney. The artist Nicole Eisenman provided a key link between these two groups and an important model for the younger generation. Among the artists

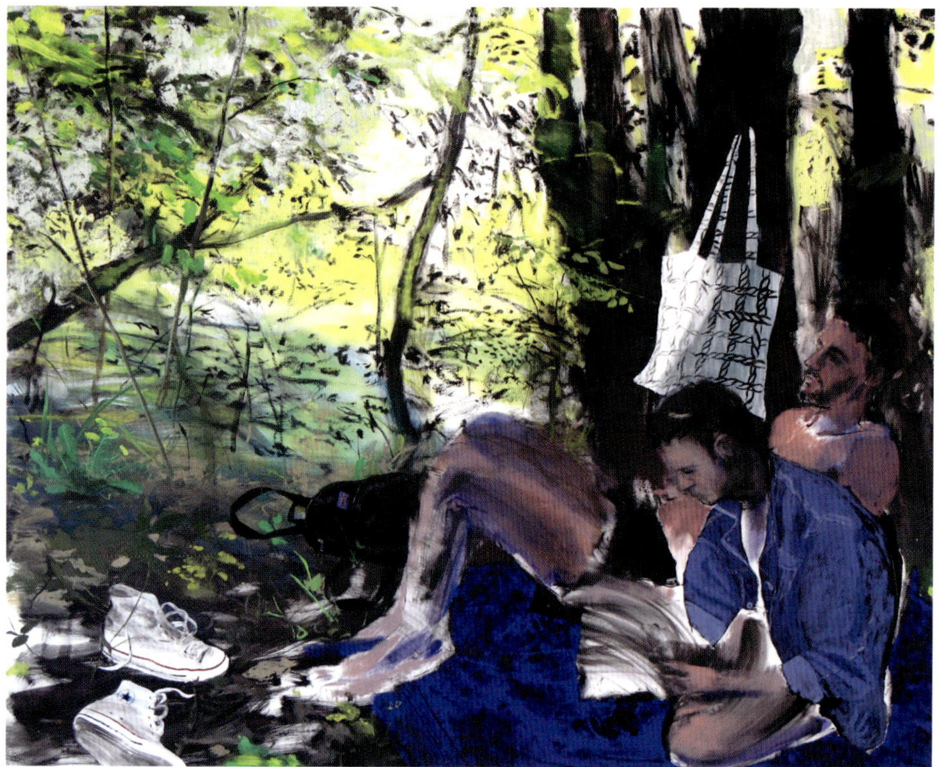

Fig. 1. Doron Langberg, *By the Lake with Emre*, 2018. Oil on canvas, 80 × 96 in. (203.2 × 243.8 cm). Private collection

represented—all born between the late 1970s and early 1990s—were Elijah Burgher, TM Davy, Louis Fratino, Sholem Krishtalka, Samantha Nye, and Michael Stamm. One particular work captivated me: Doron Langberg's *By the Lake with Emre* (fig. 1). Confronted with a Queer *Déjeuner sur l'herbe*, I was spellbound. Stephen's exhibition was not the first to feature Queer figuration, but thanks to him I was introduced to a world of Queer art with more power than anything I had encountered before. Later exhibitions, meetings, and studio visits introduced me to the work of Kyle Coniglio, Jenna Gribbon, Toyin Ojih Odutola, Jennifer Packer, and Salman Toor. The last three have been the focus of superb exhibitions at the Whitney Museum of American Art: *Toyin Ojih Odutola: To Wander Determined* (2017–18), *Salman Toor: How Will I Know* (2020–21), and *Jennifer Packer: The Eye Is Not Satisfied with Seeing* (2021–22). Not only did most of these artists—Queer themselves or choosing to represent predominantly Queer subjects—elect to work within the realm of figuration in painting, but many of them, as I learned in getting to know them over the past few years, are deeply interested in Old Master paintings and specifically in the works at the Frick.

In conjunction with Stephen Truax and Aimee Ng, the idea of commissioning four works to display at Frick Madison emerged as we were considering what to hang in the galleries when four masterpieces from the collection—coincidentally all by northern European artists—would be on loan to exhibitions. Johannes Vermeer's *Girl Interrupted at Her Music* traveled to the Gemäldegalerie in Dresden for a Vermeer exhibition, Holbein's *Thomas Cromwell* and *Sir Thomas More* were lent to the J. Paul Getty Museum in Los Angeles and the Morgan Library and Museum in New York (respectively) for two iterations of a Holbein show, and Rembrandt's *Polish Rider* returned for the first time in more than a century to Poland, to be exhibited in Warsaw and Kraków. While these works temporarily left the museum, paintings by Salman Toor, Doron Langberg, Jenna Gribbon, and Toyin Ojih Odutola, respectively, were created to replace them and to be in conversation with the other works by Vermeer, Holbein, and Rembrandt in the galleries. Four painters, living and working in New York (though originally from Pakistan, Israel, Tennessee, and Nigeria), displayed their responses to masterpieces from the Frick for a year—between September 2021 and September 2022. This book is the result of that project, and it presents the works, their display at the Frick, and the responses the project engendered. In Andrew Holleran's seminal novel *Dancer from the Dance* (1978), one of the main characters writes: "Even if people accept fags out of kindness, even if they tolerate the poor dears, they don't want to know WHAT THEY DO." This new generation of Queer figurative artists in New York—and the curators working with them—believe, instead, as Frank O'Hara wrote in his "Ode to Joy" (1957): "We shall have everything we want and there'll be no more dying."

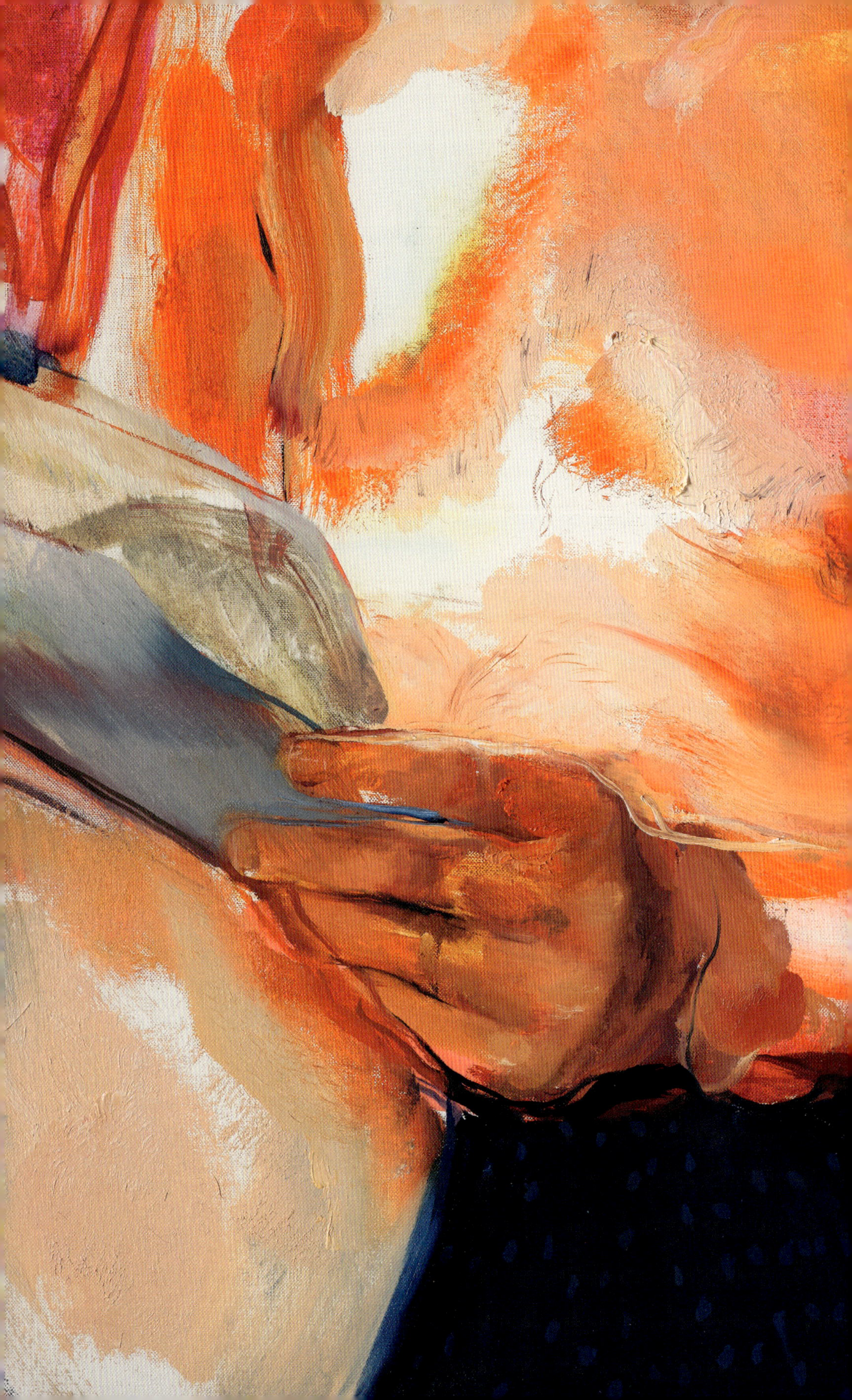

"WE CAN OCCUPY THIS SPACE NOW"

Stephen Truax

The work of Doron Langberg, Salman Toor, Jenna Gribbon, and Toyin Ojih Odutola is almost shocking in the context of The Frick Collection. Never has recent figurative painting looked so fresh as these four do adjacent to their historical predecessors.

It is ironic that figurative painting in oil, long considered reactionary and conservative, is now positioned as a radical departure from political, concept-driven art. Drawing from the legacy of feminist art, these young Queer artists reassert that the personal is political. This kind of pillow-talk painting, which would have so recently been considered solipsistic and self-indulgent, has become *de rigueur* for U.S. institutions of the highest caliber. Langberg's work was recently on view at the Rubell Museum, Miami, and the ICA Boston; Toor's at the Baltimore Museum of Art (where he went toe-to-toe with Van Dyck) and earlier at the Whitney Museum of American Art. Gribbon's work was included in *Women Painting Women*, curated by Andrea Karnes at the Modern Art Museum of Fort Worth, and Ojih Odutola's was recently on view at the Barbican Art Gallery, the Kunsten Museum of Modern Art, the Hirshhorn Museum, and also at the Whitney.

The movement has not always received such a warm reception: in 2019, Barry Schwabsky, art critic of *The Nation*, described Langberg, and contemporary Queer figurative painting in general, as "a little too wedded to history, almost unthinkingly assiduous in delving into the resources offered by figurative traditions."[1] Langberg and his colleagues have all remarked that museums are some of their greatest teachers, particularly New York institutions like the Frick. "We [artists] relate to works in major museums as friends," Langberg has said. "We know them intimately and visit them regularly. . . . We learn through direct access to the work." It is precisely here, at the Frick, embedded in a broad range of Western art, that these young artists are at

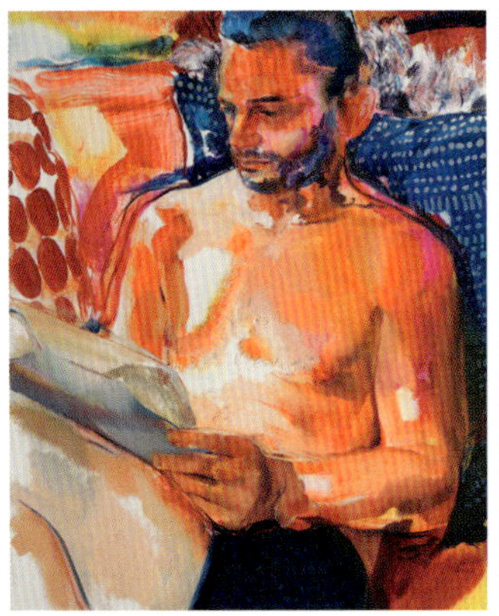

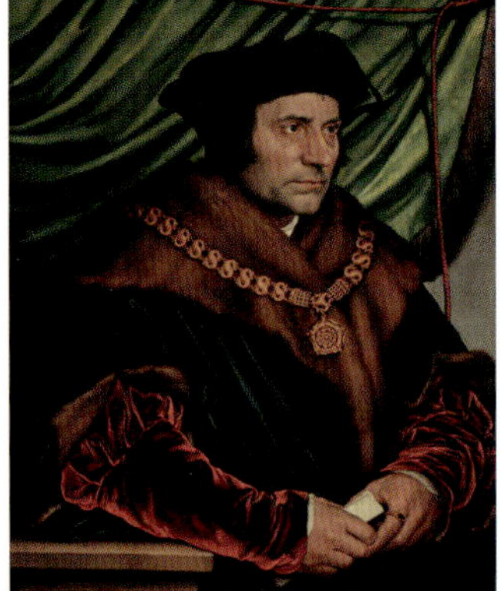

Fig. 2. Doron Langberg's *Lover* (cat. 2) and Hans Holbein the Younger's *Sir Thomas More* (fig. 16)

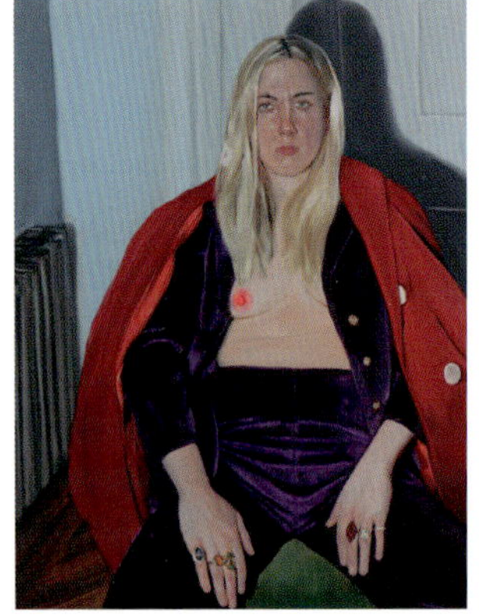

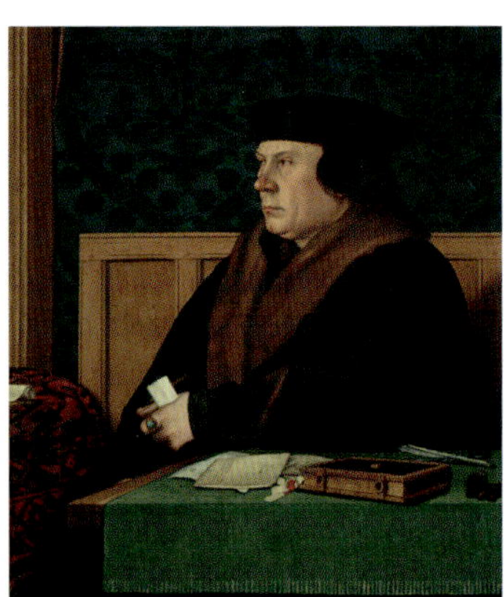

Fig. 3. Jenna Gribbon's *What Am I Doing Here? I Should Ask You the Same* (cat. 1) and Hans Holbein the Younger's *Thomas Cromwell* (fig. 10)

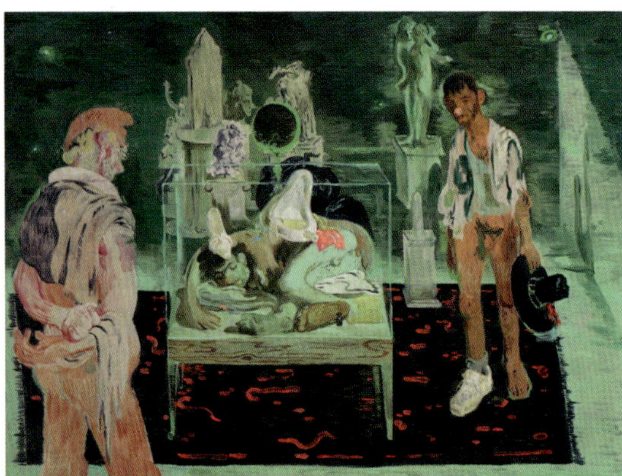

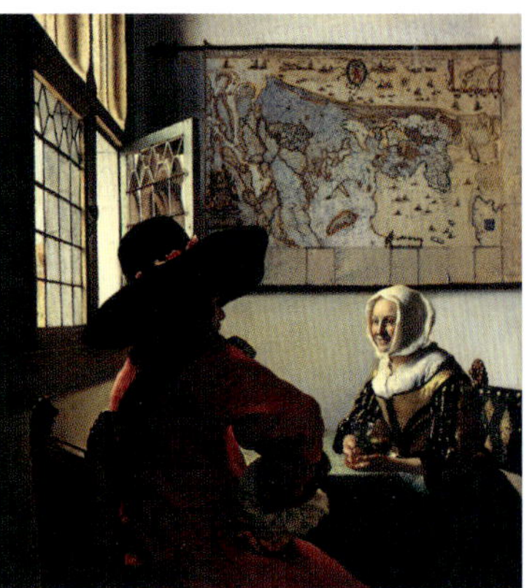

Fig. 4. Salman Toor's *Museum Boys* (cat. 3) and Johannes Vermeer's *Officer and Laughing Girl* (fig. 24)

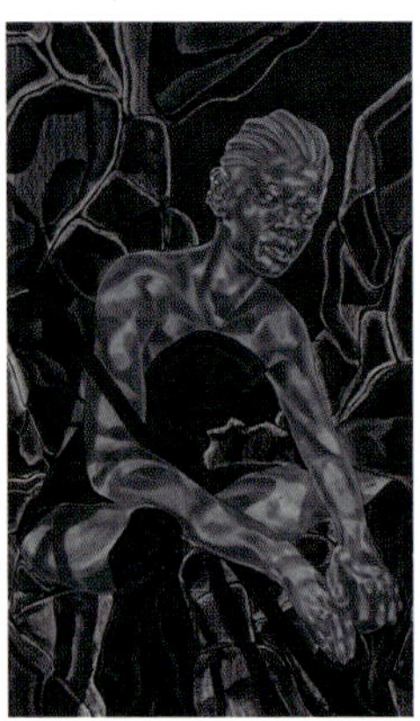

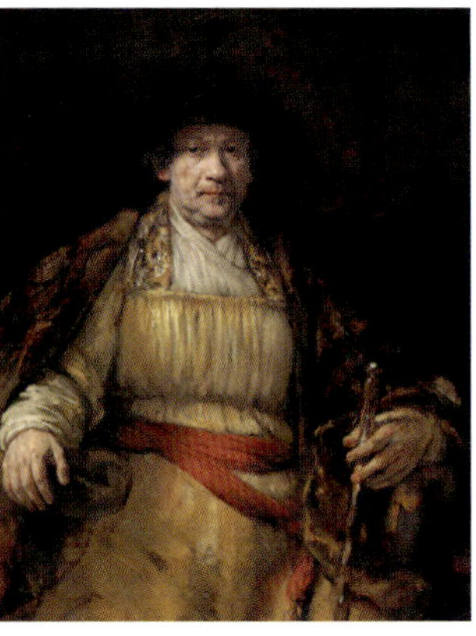

Fig. 5. Toyin Ojih Odutola's *The Listener* (cat. 4) and Rembrandt's *Self-Portrait* (fig. 29)

their most powerful because it underscores just how profoundly divergent contemporary figurative painting is from its history.

~

Naked from the waist up, the young man bares his black briefs and thigh, just visible along the bottom edge of the picture. Lamplight cascades across his chest. It is a light that the painter, Doron Langberg, achieves by leaving the primed canvas open, untouched—a nod to twentieth-century figurative painters like Alice Neel. His shoulder, arm, and hands are in shadow, illuminated only by the ambient light of the bedroom, with little more than a wash of umber, orange, and fuchsia. His pink nipple glows erotically. When Xavier Salomon asked Langberg to make a painting in response to the portrait of Sir Thomas More (see fig. 16) by Hans Holbein the Younger, and to present it adjacent to the *actual painting*, the artist knew immediately that the work he would produce "had to be located at the center of [his] practice." Langberg painted a portrait of a young man (someone who was very close to him) and gave it a title he often uses: *Lover*.

In his permanent Frick home, More stares, eternally dour, at Holbein's portrait of Thomas Cromwell (see fig. 10), who seems to glower back. The temporary reinstallation of the two works at the brutalist Breuer building (the historical site of the Whitney Museum, for which the building was designed) keeps them together in the same sheetrock-walled gallery under the building's iconic cast-concrete grid ceiling. Henry Clay Frick acquired these two portraits and paired them intentionally. He made efforts to reunite amorous couples or, in this case, enemies. It was the unprecedented loan of the Cromwell portrait to the Holbein survey at the J. Paul Getty Museum in Los Angeles that allowed for the presentation of the *Living Histories* project at all. The More portrait would later travel to the Morgan Library and Museum in New York. In Cromwell's place, Langberg allows *Lover* (cat. 2) to regard More in a similar way; *Lover*, too, faces More, albeit more distantly.

While More stares off into the future or to a higher power (the way politicians often do), posing for the official portrait that would define his legacy, Langberg's subject looks down, intently reading and seeming to ignore the fact that he is being painted at all (fig. 2). He is unnamed; we don't know who he is now, and he will bear no identity in the future. More was nearly fifty at the time the portrait was painted, whereas Langberg's subject is young and virile, perhaps in his thirties. He is marked by the kind of permanent adolescence our contemporary economy assigns to this generation. He is at once at work and in repose, a subtle nod to the nature of today's labor economy, where we find ourselves so often simultaneously working and relaxing.

Taking his lead from the More portrait, Langberg crops his composition tightly around his subject, keeps the canvas at approximately the same scale, and frames his subject's beautiful hands at the lower center of the canvas just as More's are framed. This medium-size format was a challenge for Langberg, who works comfortably oversize and plein-air on a French easel.

In his response painting, Langberg echoes several elements in the Holbein canvas: a bit of correspondence that More holds between his fingers (he was a man of letters) becomes a text printed on 8½-by-11-inch copy paper folded at a staple in the top left corner of the document, underscoring the contemporaneity of the work. A golden signet ring worn by More is, in the Langberg, a wedding band. More's five-o'clock shadow is articulated in lifelike detail, while the face of the subject in *Lover* is alight beneath a field of bright blue brushstrokes that decorate the carefully executed blue underdrawing (again, as in a Neel painting).

Holbein's More is surrounded by expensive textiles: his lush red velvet sleeve, his cowl of animal fur, a green curtain, each a different surface the feel of which we can imagine. Langberg's subject also reclines against a rich assortment of patterned pillows and blankets. The semi-transparent objects that surround him are as much brushstrokes as concrete objects, a kind of painterly shorthand for an intimate interior; at the extreme edges of the painting, they dissolve altogether.

The extraordinary specificity Holbein achieves borders on devotional, with each brown strand of hair articulated, almost etched into the surface of the oak panel. The few tightly contoured shapes fit together like puzzle pieces locked into place. Each area is so highly developed that it appears slightly raised on the painting's surface, and the boundaries between objects seem to be incised into it like an intaglio impression. Langberg, in contrast, works at speed and takes a certain amount of liberty in his gestural mark-making. Our minds fill in the rest. This portrait was made in just a few sessions.

Langberg paints thinly, applying highly pigmented oil over a white oil ground. This allows light to reflect off that white ground and project through the oil, as in a watercolor. In comparison to Holbein's traditional layering of opaque earth tones over a gray ground, the Langberg radiates color and light. During installation, the Frick had to dim down the lights on it.

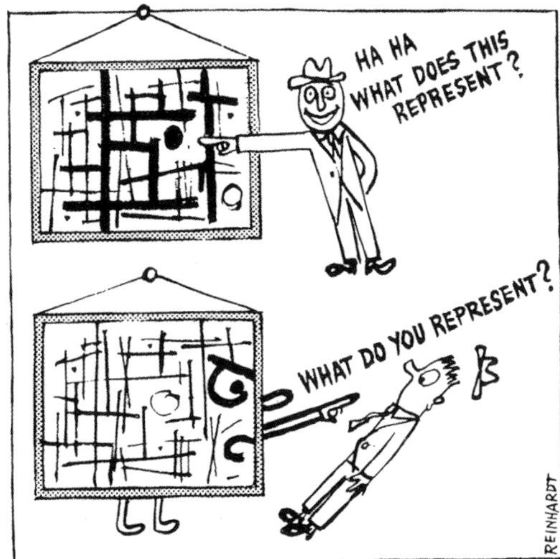

Fig. 6. Ad Reinhardt, "How to Look at a Cubist Painting." *PM,* January 27, 1946

~

Perhaps prepared in anticipation of a public backlash, Jenna Gribbon titled her response painting *What Am I Doing Here? I Should Ask You the Same* (cat. 1). Paired with Holbein's portrait of Thomas Cromwell, Gribbon's portrait of her partner, the musician Mackenzie Scott, puts the viewer in direct confrontation with her subject (fig. 3). Like the famous Ad Reinhardt cartoon in which an abstract painting confronts its accusatory viewer (fig. 6), Mackenzie locks eyes with us, daring us to say something.

Gribbon says she imagined Mackenzie sitting in the room with Cromwell, an older (straight) white man in an obvious position of power. She imagined her lover would have sat just like this in front of him; her face in a scowl (just as Cromwell scowls), her legs spread open defiantly. Despite this antagonistic relationship between the two artists' subjects, Gribbon says the painting is "a love letter to Holbein." Gribbon fixates on the luxurious textiles throughout the painting. Mackenzie wears a purple velvet suit over her shirtless torso: Gribbon's effort to "crank up the camp nature of Holbein," and an adaptation of Cromwell's fabulous fur-lined velvet robe.

In this portrait, Mackenzie, an overtly Queer-identified woman, intentionally takes up space; her body dominates most of the composition. Her breast is exposed like the goddess Diana in Titian's *Death of Actaeon*. In this painting, Diana orders Actaeon to be devoured by his own hounds as punishment for surprising the goddess and her nymphs, who suffered under his male gaze. The three-quarter-length portrait of Mackenzie towering at four feet tall makes the figure larger than life and certainly larger than Cromwell. The harsh light from a clamp light (familiar from other images in Gribbon's oeuvre) gives Mackenzie's flesh and clothes an eerie, luminous quality. It is not hard to imagine Mackenzie as powerful and furious as a god.

~

In Salman Toor's native Pakistan, men hold hands, walk with their arms around each other's shoulders, and rest their hands on each other's thighs, perhaps while waiting for a train. Although homosexuality is still not accepted, physical touch between men is very common. It can also encode homosociality, and this slippage has been an ongoing subject for the young painter. Art historians have suggested that Vermeer similarly encoded his images, as in *Officer and Laughing Girl* (see fig. 24). It was uncommon for a man, especially an officer of high station, to have a private audience with a young woman, and it has been suggested that the broad smile and open hand of Vermeer's "laughing girl" indicate that she is requesting payment before sex. Capturing this erotic undercurrent in this seemingly straightforward, formalist painting was key for Toor in his response painting, *Museum Boys* (cat. 3).

Using foreshortening, Vermeer emphasizes the dominant role of the officer by making him visually larger than the young woman, who by contrast seems more diminutive. His broad hat is adorned with extravagant red feathers, each rimmed with golden sunlight. Toor positions a figure, the color of "bacon," on the left, his back to the viewer (just as in *Officer and Laughing Girl*), and also makes him physically larger using foreshortening. On the right, instead of the laughing girl, we find a beautiful brown man naked from the waist down and holding a familiar black hat adorned with red feathers (fig. 4).

Drawing directly from Western art-historical sources is a common aspect of Toor's practice. "I never felt like I was stealing by looking at and loving these images," Toor said in a recent interview. He structures his work on Western art history; his early independent education was spent in the most important collections in London, Paris, and New York. While these museums represent Western empire, and the concentration of wealth and power in Europe and the United States (i.e., the racist domination of the non-white world), Toor remarked simply, "I wanted to see what all that money bought." When friends asked Toor how he squared his heritage and experience with a Western art-historical form and structure—namely, one that would have rejected him, a Queer-identified artist from Pakistan—Toor responded, "I had to make peace long ago with the fact that these dead white men would have been racist toward me/us."

A finely detailed map hangs in the background behind the couple in *Officer and Laughing Girl*; Toor repositions it as a large black rectangular rug beneath his vitrine. Similar to the possibly illicit conversation in the Vermeer,

Toor's characters regard each other, and perhaps they engage in quiet, romantic communication in a museum. The relocation from a Dutch interior to a museum space underscores the economics of the contemporary art market in comparison to Vermeer's time, when artists worked primarily for wealthy patrons who would present their work in private salons. Within the vitrine between them, Toor has enclosed two young men naked and asleep in a "fag puddle"; we view Queer male sexual intimacy under glass. The couple sleeps peacefully in the vitrine under a urinal (which any art history initiate would identify as Duchamp's 1917 *Fountain* sculpture, the ultimate symbol of the avant-garde) and a high-heeled slipper. Toor makes overt what in the Vermeer is a subtle social cue.

When Salomon approached Toor with the opportunity to show alongside Vermeer, the artist told me he "literally died." Few artists in the Western canon convey the same sense of mystery or elicit the same admiration and respect as Vermeer, who has only thirty-four works attributed to him. However, Toor told me, "I was not intimidated to hang next to Vermeer. I knew I couldn't measure up." Rather than attempting to rival the master, Toor loosened his brushstrokes and made the work more casual. He told me, "It helps to be kind of 'blah' in a very formal, buttoned-up space." This looseness in execution and composition underscores the work's timeliness and links it to recent painters like Karen Kilimnik and Nicole Eisenman.

~

Though enthroned, richly attired, and holding a golden scepter, Rembrandt seems weakened by the years in the 1658 self-portrait he made just eleven years before his death. The buttery depth of the old man's visage is almost too real. Rembrandt's quick glazes achieve a more subtle, detailed, and complex portrayal than any image a camera could generate.

This fabulous example of his late self-portraits emerges candlelit and soft from a warm and spacious darkness. The figure in Toyin Ojih Odutola's *The Listener* (cat. 4) also sits on a black background, but hers is a flat, matte expanse. As crisp and resolute as a Greek frieze, the charcoal-and-pastel figure is unapologetically flat and impenetrable and towers over her company at seven feet tall. This figure emerges from Ojih Odutola's 2020–22 exhibition *A Countervailing Theory*, comprising more than forty related works also in charcoal and pastel on a black ground that detail a fictional ancient civilization of female warriors of the artist's own invention.

Glittering as if moistened by tears, Rembrandt's dark brown eyes—impossible in their depth, emotionality, and even sincerity—look directly at us, making eye contact. His expression seems to be that of someone regarding us with an old familiarity. The eyes of the figure in *The Listener* also glisten but harshly so, as she looks away from the viewer, indifferent to our presence. Her finely muscled throat, arms, and legs are all frozen in the same even, unearthly light.

Ojih Odutola offers a counterpoint to the Rembrandt: instead of aspiring to compete with him and his myth, the young artist presents her own. Rather than make a work that echoes Rembrandt's melancholy acknowledgment of his mortality, Ojih Odutola creates a warrior that seems majestic and imperturbable, luxuriating in her own youth, beauty, and strength. It flips the existing power dynamic. Rembrandt, an august white man adorned with the trappings of wealth, appears feeble, merely pretending to wield true power. In *The Listener*, Ojih Odutola's larger-than-life Black woman is resplendent in her aloofness, born to power (fig. 5).

~

With this project, The Frick Collection has exposed a wider audience to recent Queer figurative painting. While its overtly sexual imagery and leftist political messaging are familiar in downtown New York galleries, in the silent rooms of the Frick, alongside Old Master paintings, it incites a much stronger reaction. The juxtaposition creates a certain tension: its very presence in this context forces critical discussion about the rest of the museum and its collection.

The glaring absence of empowered women, of races other than white, and of artists identified as anything but heterosexual is apparent at the Frick, but the introduction of Langberg, Gribbon, Toor, and Ojih Odutola makes the issue unavoidable. By bringing into the museum Queer figurative painting's brand of sex-positivity and flamboyant representations of Queer lifestyle, this project casts a harsh light on the Frick, one that contrasts sharply with recent efforts by other U.S. museums.

The apotheosis of Queer figurative painting in museums has been fast. Just ten years ago, it would have been difficult to imagine these young painters in any museum, much less adjacent to Holbein, Rembrandt, and Vermeer. Moreover, in that short time frame, this loose association of young artists, many of whom are friends, have all achieved high prices at auction.

For all their success, these artists and Queer figurative painting in general are sometimes disregarded as preaching to the choir and derided for reinforcing traditional standards of beauty, sexuality, and body representation.

Despite the broad acceptance of this work and its commercial success in the bubble of the contemporary art world, the vitriolic response from some members of the Frick's wider audience on social media proves that this work remains urgent and timely. Langberg, Toor, Gribbon, and Ojih Odutola all suffered slanderous comments on the Frick's social-media accounts. Some of them were *ad hominem* attacks about how they spoke ("too gay"), their youth and good looks, or just their collective decision to allow their works to be shown adjacent to the Old Masters at all.

Gribbon was targeted most of all, and, as a result, Mackenzie took to Instagram to clap back at her detractors. Responses to a photograph of the artist standing next to her painting included one comment that was just a nauseous emoji. Mackenzie responded, "I felt the same when I saw your profile image." "Alright enough with this 'art' barf . . ." prompted Mackenzie's "It's good that misogynist homophobes like you reveal themselves publicly."

Negative online comments are a common issue in Gribbon's life; no other artist featured here has such a regular experience of negative public feedback. Uninformed social-media users often mistake her regular portraits of Mackenzie for self-portraits, which Gribbon suggests might be the result of the collective denial of the possibility of a woman loving another woman, or a female artist selecting a female subject as her muse. It remains just as problematic to be a woman artist as it does to be a Queer-identified artist.

But *Living Histories* at the Frick forces the issue and asks: What is the role of the Queer artist in the world? For such a project to take place at the Frick, these four artists not only went "once more unto the breach, dear friends" but perhaps accidentally embarked toward a new horizon. The result was a bit uncomfortable, as even an audience as genteel as one would expect to find at the Frick still offered resistance. But to be seen in the context of the works that inspired them, Langberg, Toor, Gribbon, and Ojih Odutola all reached not only a greater, deeper relationship with art history but created a more profound space for meaning in their practice. At the conclusion of a panel discussion held for the project, Toor said, "We can occupy this space now."

Note

1. Barry Schwabsky, "What's Wrong with the New Figurative Painting?" *The Nation*, October 30, 2019, https://www.thenation.com/article/archive/whats-wrong-with-the-new-figurative-painting/.

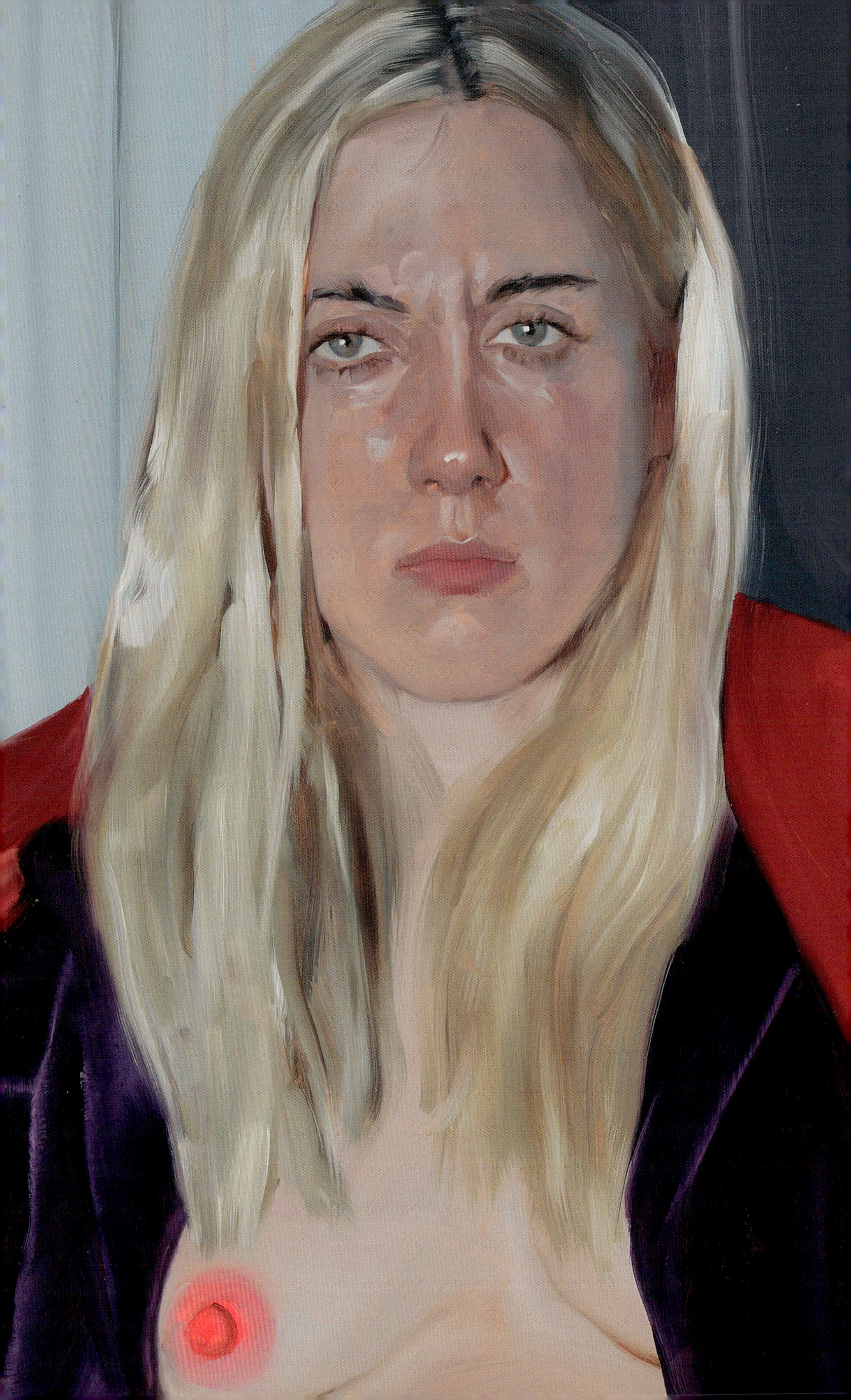

JENNA GRIBBON AND TOYIN OJIH ODUTOLA: COLOR AS COMMUNIQUÉ

Jessica Bell Brown

For Jenna Gribbon and Toyin Ojih Odutola, color is a pronouncement of sorts. It unlocks a strategic mode of communication that is about being seen and being recognized—a specific foray into a representational world not set apart from the world of the Old Masters but implicated in a system of value, position, and art-historical recognition. Color conveys symbolic power. It conveys emotional or psychological charge, and, like Fra Angelico's lapis lazuli or Judd's cadmium red, hues carry a material history and value that make works of art all the more complex conceptually and socially. Artists employ color as a means to control the picture; color provides both access to the world they have built and a re-entry point into the world that we as viewers inhabit. It establishes the preconditions of belief, of verisimilitude, or, in some cases, of dysmorphia. Through subtle shifts in value or tone, one can match a material expression to a corresponding feeling or emotion. These possibilities have stood the test of time, from the oldest creative utterances to the most contemporary paintings hanging in a Chelsea gallery.

Gribbon's work offers an object lesson in the ways that color can convey the subtle dynamics of power, not unlike in its companion painting, Holbein's portrait of English Reformationist and lawyer Thomas Cromwell, Earl of Essex. Modes of dress, possessions, and environs intricately arranged and messaged are all dynamics of representation that are often unstable, requiring viewers to believe in the value propositions of the works and meanings. Since the inception of painting, color has been about luxury—color as an economy of expression. In her arresting portrait *What Am I Doing Here? I Should Ask You the Same* (cat. 1), a mélange of textures and colors suggests a system of contrast—precious jewel tones that contrast with her subject, Mackenzie, the artist's partner. Mackenzie gazes directly at the viewer as she sits on an upholstered velvety green chair, a sliver of which is exposed by her spread legs. Gribbon drapes her lover's body with a violet suit and crimson jacket, also velvet in texture. With her shirtless subject, Gribbon signals a palpable masculine sensibility that she countersignals with a single exposed breast, from the center of which protrudes an unnaturalistic neon-pink nipple. The nipple, the fulcrum of the image, holds the seductive and illusory power of color in image-making. A faint gray shadow behind the sitter heightens the sense of a double presence (of viewer and sitter) in the realm of the painting. This portrait embraces symmetry and at the same time skews it slightly in order to Queer it. Mackenzie's bare chest calls attention to a gaze that all too often makes depictions of female bodies bend to the will and pleasure of their renderers. In a 2018 interview for *The Last Magazine*, Gribbon succinctly describes the relational conceit of her work:

> My paintings have a certain familiar appeal . . . pretty colors, beautiful women in what might appear to be seductive scenarios. But they're also Trojan horses in a way; you're drawn in and you expect to be able to interact with the subjects of the painting in the familiar modern or pre-modern way, but then when you actually begin to see what's depicted, you have to address issues of agency, consent, and the relationship between the artist and viewer.[1]

Gribbon paints her lover's expressivity with casual naturalism and, at the same time, dresses her with maximalist sartorial embellishment to raise important questions: Who gets to be vibrant? Who gets to be bold? Who receives luxurious treatment in paint, while others receive minimal consideration? Mackenzie occupies a space often reserved in Renaissance portraits for royalty and elites. Her skin is pale and milky white. Amid superfluousness and exuberance, her facial expression carries a furrowed brow. Gribbon as a painter is not in lockstep with the enterprise of reifying an archetypal female subject. Her disobedience to the trope of the supine or "directed" feminine muse captured by a great male painter is what makes *What Am I Doing Here? I Should Ask You the Same* utterly provocative.

Taking advantage of the refinement and austerity of a monochrome palette—developed from a black ground on linen—Ojih Odutola's *The Listener* (cat. 4) works in stark contrast to Gribbon's expansive color palette. *The Listener* is a larger-than-life-size portrait drawing in which every subtle gesture of the hand is pronounced through tones of gray and black. We see a figure, seated in deep contemplation, amid a throne of rocks and boulders that cascade down the drawing's surface. Where we experience a kind of verticality of the formation—inspired by a geological rock formation in Plateau State, Nigeria—the figure's arduously rendered gray skin stretches across the expanse of the work, almost echoing the topography that surrounds her. Ojih Odutola creates skin that shimmers like light dancing on water. Her subject's body is slender and toned, dressed efficiently for movement and agility. Androgyny and the monochrome palette are twinned devices that effectively move us from expedient consumers of the drawing to being made complicit in a world not of our making. We are absorbed into a "drawn, inverted chalky economy"[2] that creates new kinds of relationships, with terms that the work creates through the juxtaposition of modes of drawing and tonal shifts. The figure holds a staff; her body is adorned with jeweled cuffs. Cumulatively, her accoutrements and environs are arguably more expressive than she. Yet her stoicism is still information—she does not meet our eyes. We are at once physically near and psychologically distant. In approaching *The Listener*, how do you come into the picture plane? What does a monochromatic approach to figural representation yield? Ojih Odutola transgresses against the idea that gray is the absence of color. Through the monochrome, she offers a sort of democratic priming for the subject she depicts.

Ojih Odutola's work takes inspiration from the artist's fictive world of pre-colonial Nigeria, a warrior ruling class called the Eshu. Created as part of *A Countervailing Theory*, a series of works commissioned by the Barbican Art Gallery in London, *The Listener* unveils a society in which power is held by women; the men, the Koba, are subservient to them. In this world of Ojih Odutola's creation, Queerness is as endemic as heterosexuality is hegemonically normalized in current society. The most vivid details rest with the vibrancy of narrative that creates the preconditions of experiencing and connecting to this work installed in the context of Old Master painters like Rembrandt at the Frick. Ojih Odutola has contributed a contemporary work that reimagines a period of time and civic accomplishment in Nigeria that precedes European colonization. Her inclusion thrusts upon the already charged space of the museum an alternative model of history, societal relations, and aesthetics.

As for the title of the work, to listen is to be consciously and actively receptive, to exercise restraint. To maintain one's sense of grounded interiority is what Kevin Quashie theorizes as the notion of "quiet" and its relationship to one's sovereignty and sense of being:

> quiet . . . is a metaphor for the full range of one's inner life—one's desires, ambitions, hungers, vulnerabilities, fears. The inner life is not apolitical or without social value, but neither is it determined entirely by publicness. In fact, the interior—dynamic and ravishing—is a stay against the dominance of the social world; it has its own sovereignty.[3]

Quietude, by nature an expression that is not verbal, becomes a radical act of self-possession, especially in a contemporary sphere that promotes an asymmetry between the value of Black life and the hypersaturation, proliferation, and circulation of Black bodies in the visual and cultural economy. To evoke the role of the speaker and listener in a visual system builds in a politics of refusal and withholding. The artist discusses this idea of the power in quietude in her commentary on the painting: "I'm thinking about the ways in which we can directly engage in purposeful confrontation and building; how to hold space for multiple perspectives within our vast, evolving world. Choosing to be quiet is its own defiant power, and to let others speak isn't a small courtesy, it's an act of sovereignty."[4]

Gribbon's and Ojih Odutola's works offer an opportunity to reflect on the ways in which color becomes a strategic mode of communication. Some passages resoundingly trumpet reclamations of power, autonomy, and self-possession. And at times, other passages and moments of description quietly whisper about the mechanism of representation itself, shot through with complexity, contradiction, and possibly, even, the faith that some semblance of transformation could be possible by seeing anew.

Notes

1. Interview with Kevin Greenberg, *The Last Magazine*, April 17, 2018, https://thelast-magazine.com/jenna-gribbon-painter-interview/.
2. Toyin Ojih Odutola, commentary for audio tour, https://www.frick.org/living_histories.
3. Kevin Quashie, *The Sovereignty of Quiet: Beyond Resistance in Black Culture* (New Brunswick, NJ, 2012), 6.
4. Toyin Ojih Odutola, commentary for audio tour, https://www.frick.org/living_histories.

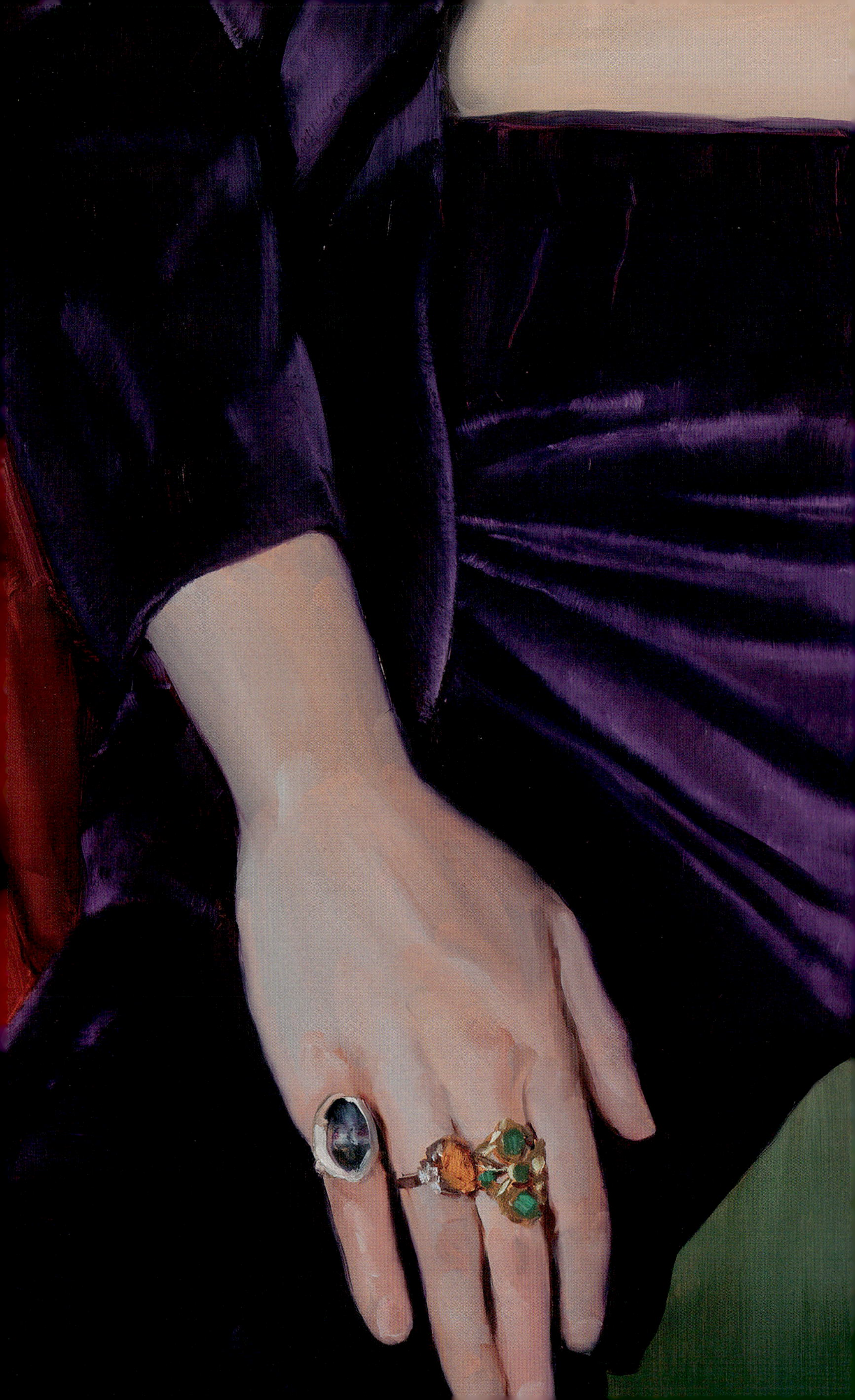

HINDSIGHT

Aimee Ng

The history of European art, particularly the Italian Renaissance, is rich with examples of same-sex desire. Its most famous artists, Leonardo da Vinci and Michelangelo, are known to have had relationships with men. Twice accused of sodomy in 1476 (with charges dropped due to no witnesses being willing to come forward), Leonardo was involved for years with a young man known as "Salaì" (translated by some as "little devil").[1] Michelangelo wrote love poems addressed to men; the artist's grandnephew, Michelangelo Buonarroti the Younger, published them after the artist's death with male pronouns changed to female, a pretense of heterosexuality that persisted until the nineteenth century.[2] Since the 1980s, scholars have expanded this area of study to include more early modern art and artists across Europe, with the crucial caveat that there are no simple parallels in any of these historical contexts to modern conceptions of homosexuality (a term first used in English in 1892), much less of "Queerness," which was reappropriated from an offensive slang term in the 1980s to encompass individuals identifying on expanded gender and sexual-orientation axes. Language used today simply does not apply directly to early modern same-sex experiences.[3]

The homoerotic elements of Leonardo's and Michelangelo's biographies have hardly become dominant features of books or exhibitions about them. Nor should they be, some might argue, for to sensationalize such aspects would distract from the art. But it is worth keeping in mind that all of the early modern European artists mentioned in this text, from the Renaissance onward, lived in times and places in which same-sex intercourse was outlawed and punishable by consequences as severe as execution. As Xavier F. Salomon notes in this publication (p. 17), this remains true in parts of the world today. In 1533—the year Holbein was painting Thomas Cromwell's portrait, some six years after he painted Thomas More's—the English Parliament passed the Buggery Act, making the "detestable & abominable vice of buggery" a felony punishable by death.[4]

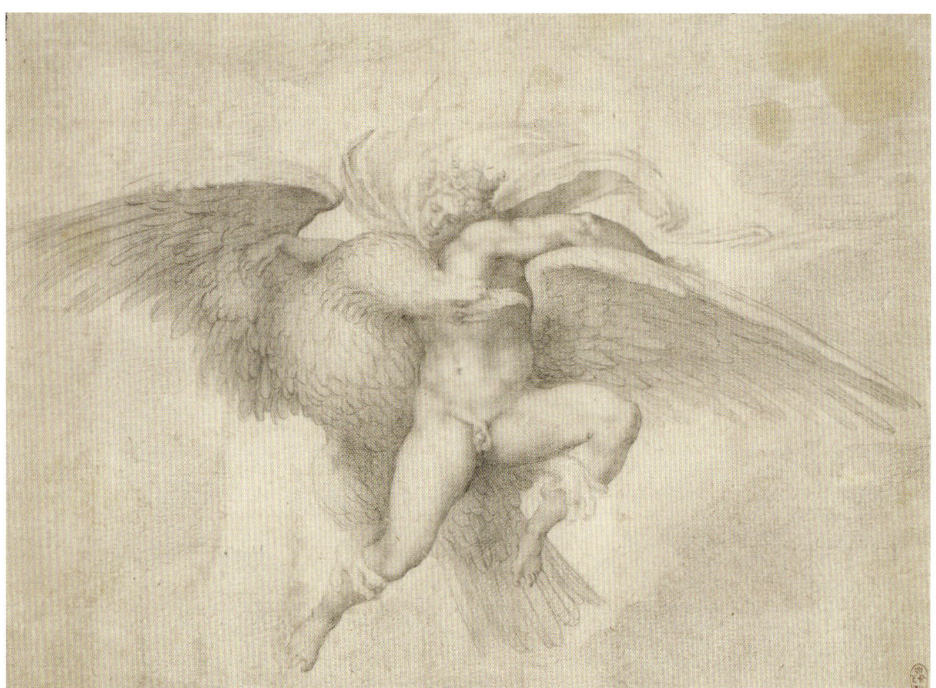

Fig. 7. Giulio Clovio after Michelangelo, *Rape of Ganymede*, ca. 1540(?). Black chalk, 7 9⁄16 × 10 ¼ in. (19.2 × 26 cm). Royal Collection Trust, London

It is no surprise that there are no monumental paintings depicting men coupling with men in early modern Europe. What survives are scant, somewhat ambiguous objects that touch upon same-sex desire indirectly, such as Michelangelo's *Rape of Ganymede* (fig. 7), a drawing of intimate scale given to Tommaso dei Cavalieri (to whom the artist addressed a number of poems), depicting one man's desire for another through the mythological scene of Jupiter, in the form of an eagle, clutching the limbs of Ganymede as he abducts him into his divine realm.[5] Another is a mysterious triple portrait, probably painted in the 1570s, believed by some to depict three *mignons* ("minions," male favorites and lovers of the king who sometimes dressed in women's clothing) of Henry III of France (fig. 8). Rumors about the privileges the king granted to his *mignons* and the way they comported themselves—including sexual activities with the king—may have contributed to Henry's assassination in 1589.[6]

Under a title that conjoins "Old Masters" with "Queer views," the *Living Histories* project prompts reflection on the myriad perspectives brought by modern audiences of historical art. The pairing of paintings by Holbein, Vermeer, and Rembrandt with works by Jenna Gribbon, Doron Langberg, Toyin Ojih Odutola, and Salman Toor is not meant to suggest that the Old

Masters or their art directly engaged with same-sex love and desire. Rather, these juxtapositions pay tribute to twenty-first-century perspectives—with emphasis on issues of gender and Queer identity that have long been marginalized in European art history—and to the significance of historical art to artists today. These pairings also inspire new ways of looking at the centuries-old paintings, some of which are explored in this essay.

~

In *Lover* (cat. 2), Doron Langberg presents his male subject through the lens of his own desire as a Queer man, giving the viewer the opportunity to see the subject as he did. Langberg's emphatic brushstrokes underscore his mediation of the beholder's view of the subject, every brushstroke a declaration of the artist's role as creator. To look again at Holbein's *Sir Thomas More* (see fig. 16) with Langberg's experiments in mind brings to the fore the concept of subjectivity—individual identity and interiority—and how wholly foreign it would have been to Holbein and his sitters. Moreover, for Holbein, the pursuit of mimesis, the convincing portrayal of a subject, was at the same time an effacing of the artist's presence. In Holbein's meticulous depiction of his

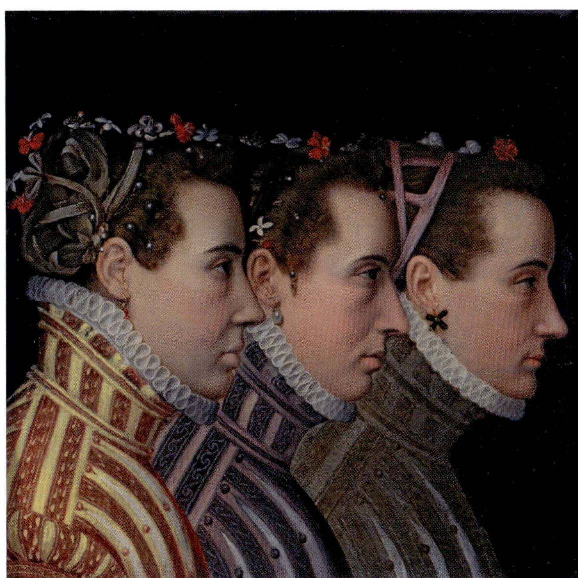

Fig. 8. School of Fontainebleau, *Triple Profile Portrait (The Mignons of Henry III)*, 1570s. Oil on slate, 22 ½ × 22 ½ in. (57.1 × 57.1 cm). Milwaukee Art Museum; Gift of the Woman's Exchange

subjects, the evidence of his own hand is eliminated, brushstrokes blurred to become the illusion itself, paint no longer paint but a fresh sprout of stubble from Thomas More's chin.

Jenna Gribbon's *What Am I Doing Here? I Should Ask You the Same* (cat. 1) offers a rebuttal to Holbein's symbols of patriarchal power in *Sir Thomas More* and *Thomas Cromwell* (see fig. 10). The portrait of her female partner encourages reflection on the roles of portraiture in Holbein's time and the different functions of portraits of men and women. *Sir Thomas More* and *Thomas Cromwell* are celebrations of the sitters, the illusion of their lifelikeness a commemoration of their individuality. They stand in contrast to some of Holbein's female portraits. The artist was charged with portraying prospective brides for Henry VIII, and in these the balance of likeness and idealization was fraught. Famously, in Holbein's portrait of Anne of Cleves, his interpretation of her was her ruin; it convinced the king to take her as his bride, but he was disappointed when he met her in person. After six months, he annulled their marriage as unconsummated. For a woman like Anne of Cleves, her actual appearance became a betrayal of the idea put forth by Holbein's brush. Gribbon's painting draws attention to the other side of Holbein's convincing portrayals in *Sir Thomas More* and *Thomas Cromwell.*

Salman Toor's *Museum Boys* (cat. 3) explores the coded body language required to communicate covertly, stemming from Toor's experience as a Queer man in conservative contexts like that of his native country, Pakistan. He sees corollaries in Vermeer's paintings, in which men and women pose in ways that leave modern viewers to wonder about the precise narratives of his pictures (for example, scholars have debated whether Vermeer's *Officer and Laughing Girl* (see fig. 24) presents a flirting couple or a transaction between a prostitute and patron). The pairing of Toor and Vermeer underscores the eloquence of human bodies and at the same time the shifting significance of gestures from one context to another. This extends to objects in the paintings: in *Museum Boys,* a bottle of poppers (a popular Queer party drug)—like the blue and white ceramic ewer (of Chinese origin modified with a European silver lid) in Vermeer's *Girl Interrupted at Her Music* (see fig. 26)—is recognizable to viewers with knowledge of these objects but foreign and possibly invisible to those without. A historical note: although comparatively few men were charged with sodomy in the Netherlands in the seventeenth century (possibly in an effort to deny its existence as a problem), great numbers were prosecuted in Utrecht in 1730, with investigators sent to uncover the men's sites of meeting and to learn the coded body language they used to communicate.[7] Looking at Vermeer through Toor's painting raises questions about the Dutch artist's interest in the legibility of his pictures and who his viewers were.

Toyin Ojih Odutola's *The Listener* (cat. 4) underscores the power of artists to manipulate fact and fiction. Her elaborate invented history for *The Listener*—the pretense of it being a printed scan of an image-bearing rock tablet found in Africa, a relic of an ancient civilization ruled by Queer Black women—draws attention to the myths of Rembrandt's portraits. Its pairing at the Frick especially with Rembrandt's *Self-Portrait* (see fig. 29), an illusion of power and authority created two years after the artist declared bankruptcy, raises questions of why and for whom he made the larger-than-life portrait of himself, seemingly enthroned as if a king, using such quantities of canvas that two pieces had to be sewn together. The early ownership of the *Self-Portrait* is unknown. Rembrandt may have produced portraits like this to sell to previous collectors of his art. Viewers of Ojih Odutola's *The Listener* are made aware of its fictions simply by looking at the drawing's surface, which bears the marks of the artist's application of chalk, pastel, and charcoal. Whether or not the first owners of Rembrandt's *Self-Portrait* appreciated the distance between its portrayal of him and his biographical reality is unknown. To modern eyes, the portrait prompts reflection on Rembrandt's self-presentation, and it is hard to reconcile such ideas of selfhood—which may have been totally alien to the artist and his time—with the prospect of simply selling an image of himself as a commodity, an object on the market that could fetch a higher price for a larger size.

~

The "Queer views" of this project derive from the perspectives of four artists in the years around 2021 and 2022. No doubt, this project and these pairings would be very different fifty years from now; and it is a presentation nearly impossible to imagine taking place fifty years ago. Over the course of this year-long project, language around Queerness, gender, and identity continued to be debated, evolving as people tried to capture the complexity of human experience.

Every viewer of a historical work of art brings something new to the encounter. From those approaching the object in the days, weeks, or months after its making to those viewing it years, decades, or centuries later, even farther removed in time and place from its original context, each individual starts a new conversation with the object. And each of these conversations enriches the work of art, broadens the possibilities of its interpretation, its ability to move people. In a way, this is the charge of public museums today: to connect art with people, to make centuries-old bits of history come alive for fresh eyes.

Notes

1. Walter Isaacson, *Leonardo da Vinci* (New York, 2017), 68–69, 131–33.
2. James M. Saslow, *The Poetry of Michelangelo: An Annotated Translation* (New Haven, 1991).
3. Indeed, the definition of "sodomy" also varied from one context to another: though prosecutions most often referred to men having intercourse with men, in various historical contexts—far from today's understanding of the term—it could also include any sex acts between men and women that were not reproductive, acts that included animals and sex with Turks, Muslims, and Jews. For this and for the general invisibility of female homoeroticism in European history, see Jonas Roelens, "Visible Women: Female Sodomy in the Late Medieval and Early Modern Southern Netherlands (1400–1550)," *Low Countries Historical Review* 130–33 (2015): 3–24 (14–15).
4. "The Buggery Act 1533," https://www.bl.uk/collection-items/the-buggery-act-1533.
5. Carmen Bambach, *Michelangelo: Divine Draftsman & Designer*, exh. cat. (Metropolitan Museum of Art, New York, 2017–18), 135–53.
6. Judith Walker Mann, in *Paintings on Stone: Science and the Sacred 1530–1800*, ed. Judith Walker Mann, exh. cat. (Saint Louis Art Museum, 2020), no. 35. See also Katherine B. Crawford, "Love, Sodomy, and Scandal: Controlling the Sexual Reputation of Henry III," *Journal of the History of Sexuality* 12, no. 4 (Oct. 2003): 513–42.
7. Theo van der Meer, "Sodom's Seeds in the Netherlands: The Emergence of Homosexuality in the Early Modern Period," *The Journal of Homosexuality* 34, no. 1 (1997): 1–16.

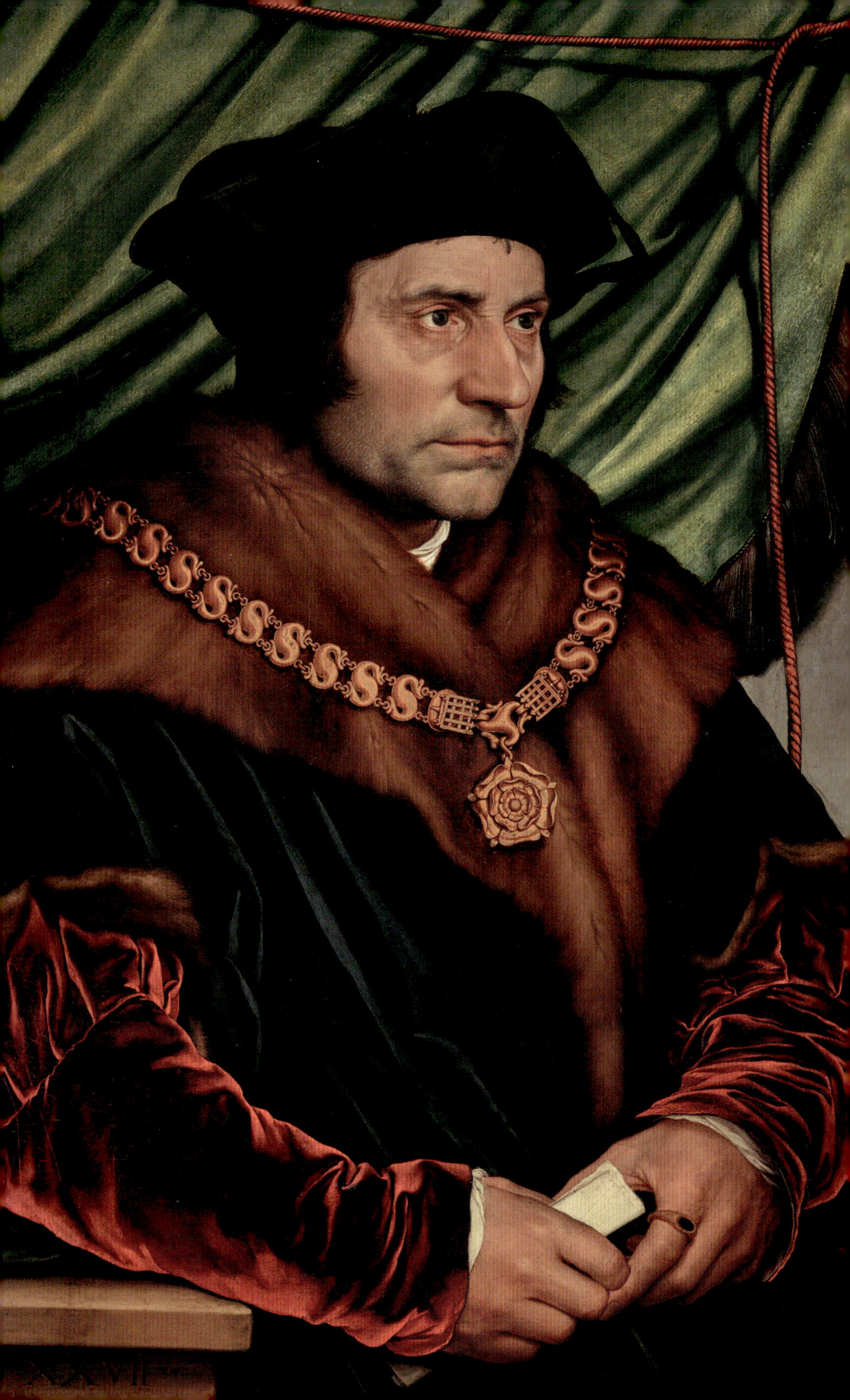

THE FUTURE EATS THE PAST, EATS THE FUTURE

Russell Tovey

The late filmmaker Derek Jarman once lamented, "If you wait long enough the world moves in circles." This summation has remained with me. It resonates with so much of contemporary existence. These "circles" come to stand for many things. For Derek, they were a critique of governmental rhetoric, the breakdown and rebirth of society, and support for and/or opposition to authentic diverse representation and opportunity. They were also an acknowledgment that marginalized communities, working in tandem, can incrementally change laws, rules, and the ill effects of indolent policies. Yet cyclical movements can also come to represent a returning narrative, presented again and again in music, fashion, and the arts. The future eats the past, eats the future.

For me, growing up, Hans Holbein was a hero, not only for being the majestic painter of majestic people but because every Holbein portrait is a historical document. A devoted history nerd, I had a Eurocentric history education that focused on the years when Holbein was most active. A preoccupation with the Tudor period—gold-star status awarded primarily to Henry VIII, in particular the despot king's back-and-forth Reformation and his switching of religions to aid in the divorcing and beheading of two of his six unfortunate wives—really tops anything any ruthless politician could ever achieve. Holbein's paintings are easily accessible in any decent Western history book; on the Internet, of course; and in a good museum collection, like the Frick. With meticulously detailed renderings, Holbein presents factual exteriors—yet not much in the way of interiors—for long-dead formidable icons. With poses proud and stances wide, they're enveloped in the finest of silk, lace, softened leather, pearls, furs, and feathers, connecting directly with the viewer or, if not, evading the viewer's gaze, stoic, cold-faced, plotting revenge and escape. But for all their coded beauty, they lack any real personality. In all of Holbein's stiff, mannered portraits, I struggle to access a semblance of the sitter's interior monologue. The information is all there, but where's the compassion? What's going on behind that folded ruff, sir? Who really are you, princess under a gable hood? Help me to help you, "Lady with a squirrel and a starling." Even your wildlife friends are cold and detached. It's hard to feel empathy for a Holbein sitter. You're impressed by them, obviously, respectful of their lofty status, but to have a connection with them on a human-to-human level is impossible. But does that really matter? Holbein is the most generous of artists, gifting us masterpieces that change our view of the past, but today I need so much more from a portrait. As a collector, I've always been drawn to the figure. And as an actor—knowing acting was my chosen career from an early age—body language, posing, and facial expressions have opened endless channels of opportunity in my own research and development, the education of my craft.

A favorite hobby was, still is, to play casting director, offering potential film roles to myself and other actors, based on the biographies of the many faces that stared out at me from the National Gallery walls. I recognize my own history in those faces, in Holbein's history, and in many of our world documenters; but when I needed a connection most, as a Queer person on the cusp of adolescence and discovery, looking into the history books for a link to the past, I didn't feel it. The history books deny us that. Holbein is better—he gives us permission to stare. To stand in front of a Holbein is a privilege. To pause at the intersection of his world and our own always troubling present raises much-needed questions. I acknowledge a privilege granted to me by a Western world that has deemed one ethnicity mainstream. It's not hard to see myself there, yet I'm troubled and saddened when it is quite the opposite for another's museum experience. We need to see ourselves in art to know each other in life.

In the context of contemporary art, we are now witnessing one of Derek's circles in full swing. Years ago, the portrait—and especially the painted portrait—was deemed a dead end. I recall being informed countless times that portraiture was over, painting people was finished, that what really mattered now was clean lines, hard edges, cold, abstracted, metallic, and expressionistic mark making. The artist was present but hiding. However, in the past three to four years, we've been witness to a renaissance of the face and a reawakening of the body that nonetheless moves away from the habitual representations of the past. Jenna Gribbon, Doron Langberg, Toyin Ojih Odutola, and Salman Toor—the four artists selected to show work at the

Frick in conversation with masterworks from the collection—are trailblazers. They are leading the way in representing what it is to truly be alive right now. Their message is universal even if their protagonists are individuals. Their work reconsiders love and empathy as assets rather than weaknesses, and a connection to their audience is far more important in the activation of their message than in any other artistic movement of the past, at least any that I am aware of. There doesn't seem to be any competitiveness among them—quite the opposite. We sense a strong alliance—united they stand, divided they fall. As contemporary painters, they joyfully circle back to Holbein and Vermeer, unashamedly citing their sources much like Holbein did when looking back to his heroes—Titian, Jan van Eyck, and Albrecht Dürer—for captivating realism and composition. But what we have now is a presentation of Queer emotion. Queer love. Queer joy. Queer empathy. A deeply authentic contemporary Queer life lived, out, proud, flawed—vulnerable and beautiful.

And yes, you also have permission to stare. Stare all you want, take all day if you'd like, be fascinated with these deeply empathetic stories because their truth has been missing from the mainstream for far too long. Bask in their vulnerabilities, engage with their flaws, and rally with them and for them in their quest for love and acceptance. In all of history, if we wait long enough, the cyclical nature of time does shift and make space; and maybe right about now, we might finally see ourselves truly represented up on those gallery walls. Like Holbein's portraits, these four artists' works are a gift of beautiful generosity, a gift for this generation, for those who follow, and for those still a twinkle twinkle. Look into their eyes, pore over their clothing, swim in their mysteries, and celebrate, for this infrequent honesty that is becoming more and more commonplace in our museums and on our gallery walls is changing the world.

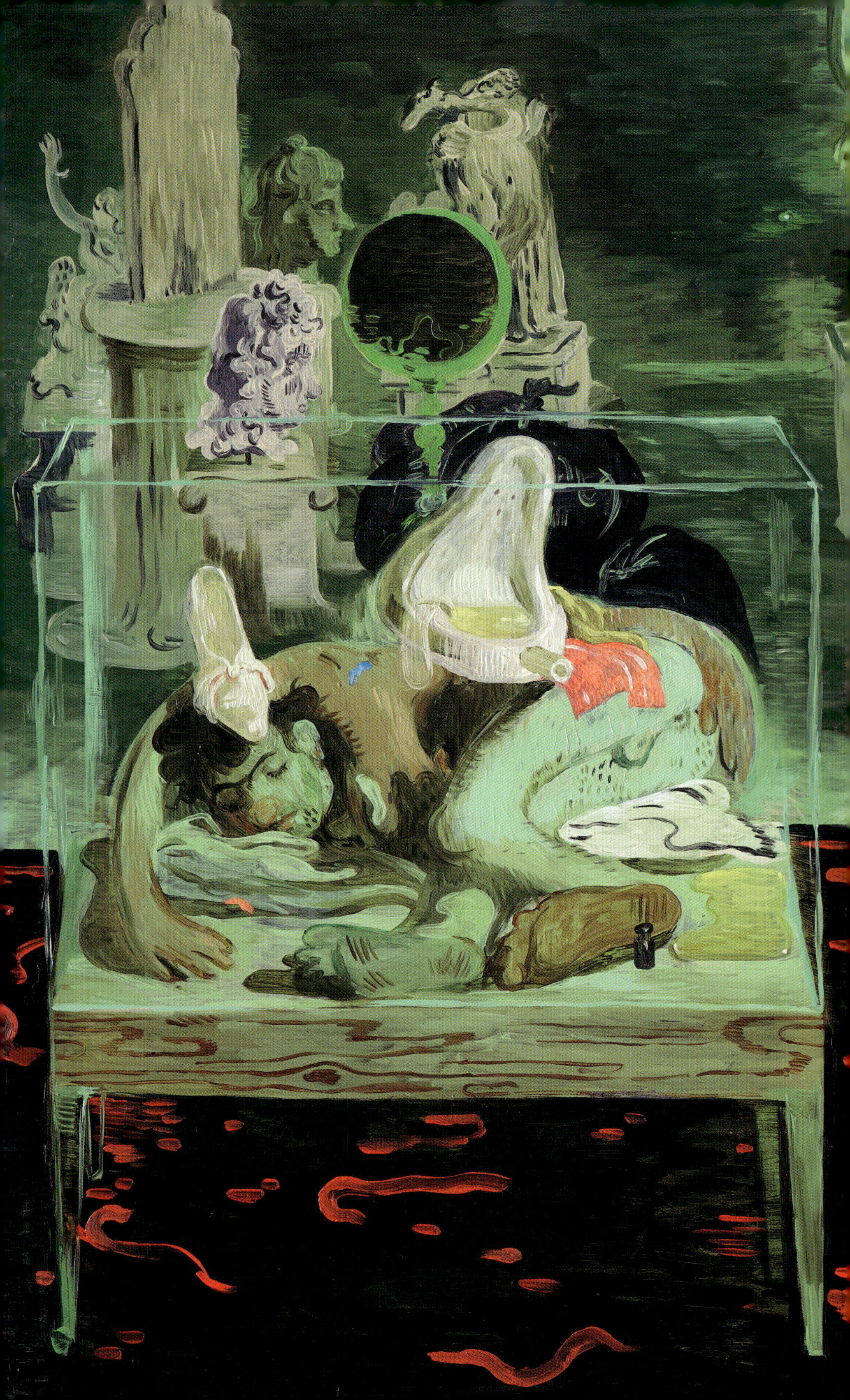

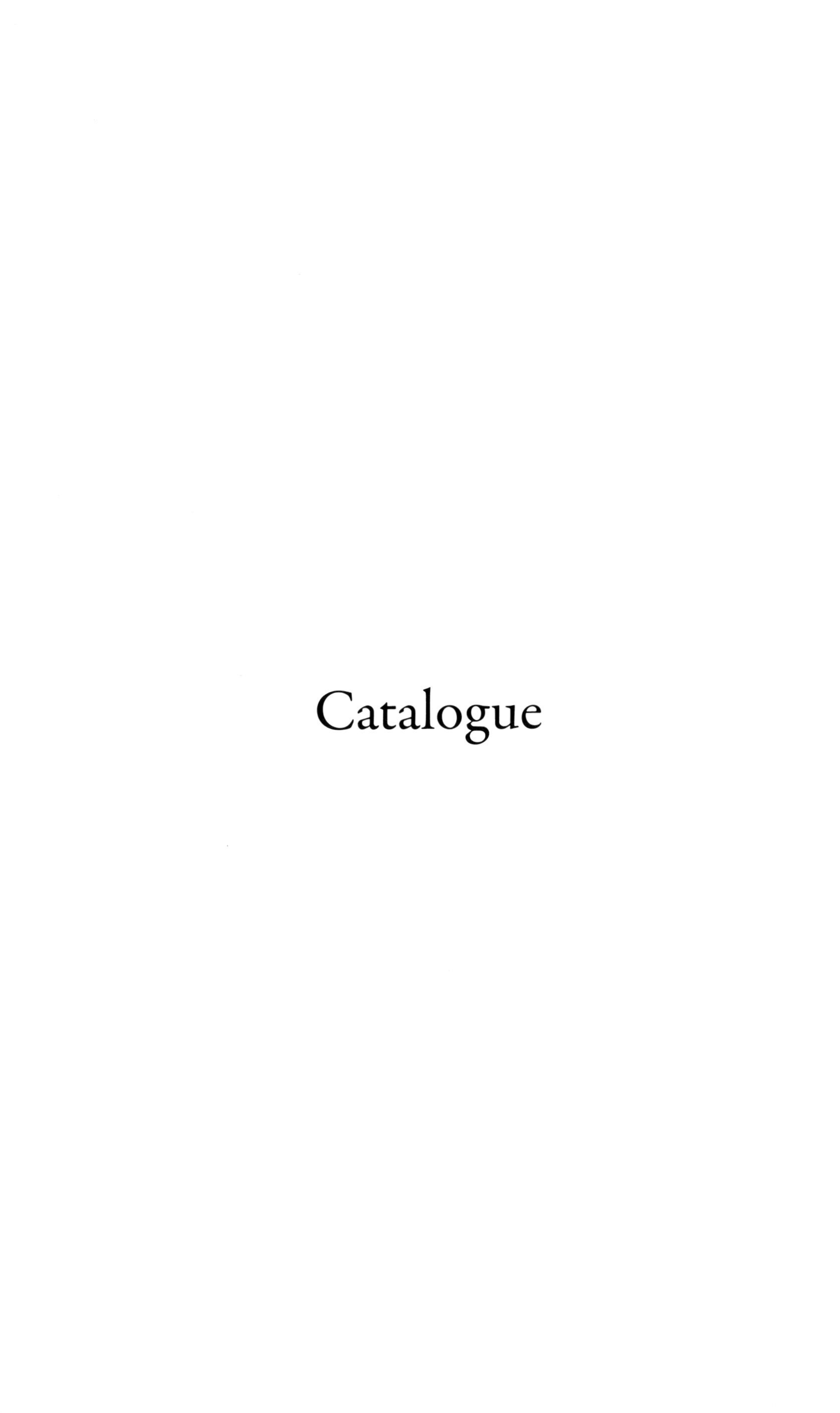

Catalogue

1

Jenna Gribbon

What Am I Doing Here? I Should Ask You the Same

2022
Oil on linen, 48 × 36 in. (121.9 × 91.4 cm)
Brant Foundation, Greenwich, Connecticut

Straw-blonde hair frames the subject's impassive face. The expression is stern, with brows furrowed and chin set, cold blue-green eyes trained forward. Flecks of white paint on the tip of the nose and around the eyes mark where the strong lamplight reflects on pink skin, while below, the flesh of the neck, breasts, and abdomen is paler, punctuated by one of Gribbon's signature neon-pink nipples and by the contours of breasts and a crease in the belly. Laid on splayed legs, two hands, each adorned with three rings, are set off against the deep purple of velvet pants, matched to the blazer above, itself encased by a red velvet coat draped over the shoulders. More velvet—the green fabric seat of the chair—forms a triangle below the figure, its apex pointing up between the legs.

The sitter is Gribbon's partner, Mackenzie, a near-constant subject in the artist's work. In the domestic setting of the home the couple share, mundane features like baby-blue walls, a radiator, and the wood floor contrast with the ostentatious and somewhat dramatic appearance of the figure. A shadow looms above, cast on the door behind. The intensity of light evokes a scene of interrogation or examination, or the blinding spotlight on an actor on stage. The subject is seated frontally and facing the viewer, like an enthroned Madonna in Christian art. In art-historical terms, the pose is called *in maestà*, meaning "in majesty." In a seated position and exposing one breast, the figure recalls the sacred image type of the Maria Lactans, the nursing Madonna (fig. 9), but without the baby and demure countenance.

Displayed at Frick Madison alongside Hans Holbein the Younger's portrait of Thomas Cromwell (fig. 10), Gribbon's painting temporarily replaced Holbein's *Sir Thomas More* (see fig. 16). The installation interrupted the century-old pairing of the two men's portraits in the Frick's galleries, their profiles facing each other as if as equals, though they were enemies. The turn of Gribbon's figure to face the viewer—rather than in profile to mirror *Thomas Cromwell*—denies a visual exchange between peers. Turning away from Cromwell, Gribbon's subject asserts a higher status and addresses the viewer. As if to mimic the tension between More's and Cromwell's portraits, Gribbon creates an exchange between Mackenzie and the viewer, complicated further by the painting's title. *What Am I Doing Here? I Should Ask You the Same* anticipates criticism and questions of validity—of the artist, subject, and beholder—and reflects the artist's consideration of individual human encounters with the painting in this gallery space. It also exposes the assumed validity and belonging of artists like Holbein and subjects like More and Cromwell in storied institutions like the Frick.

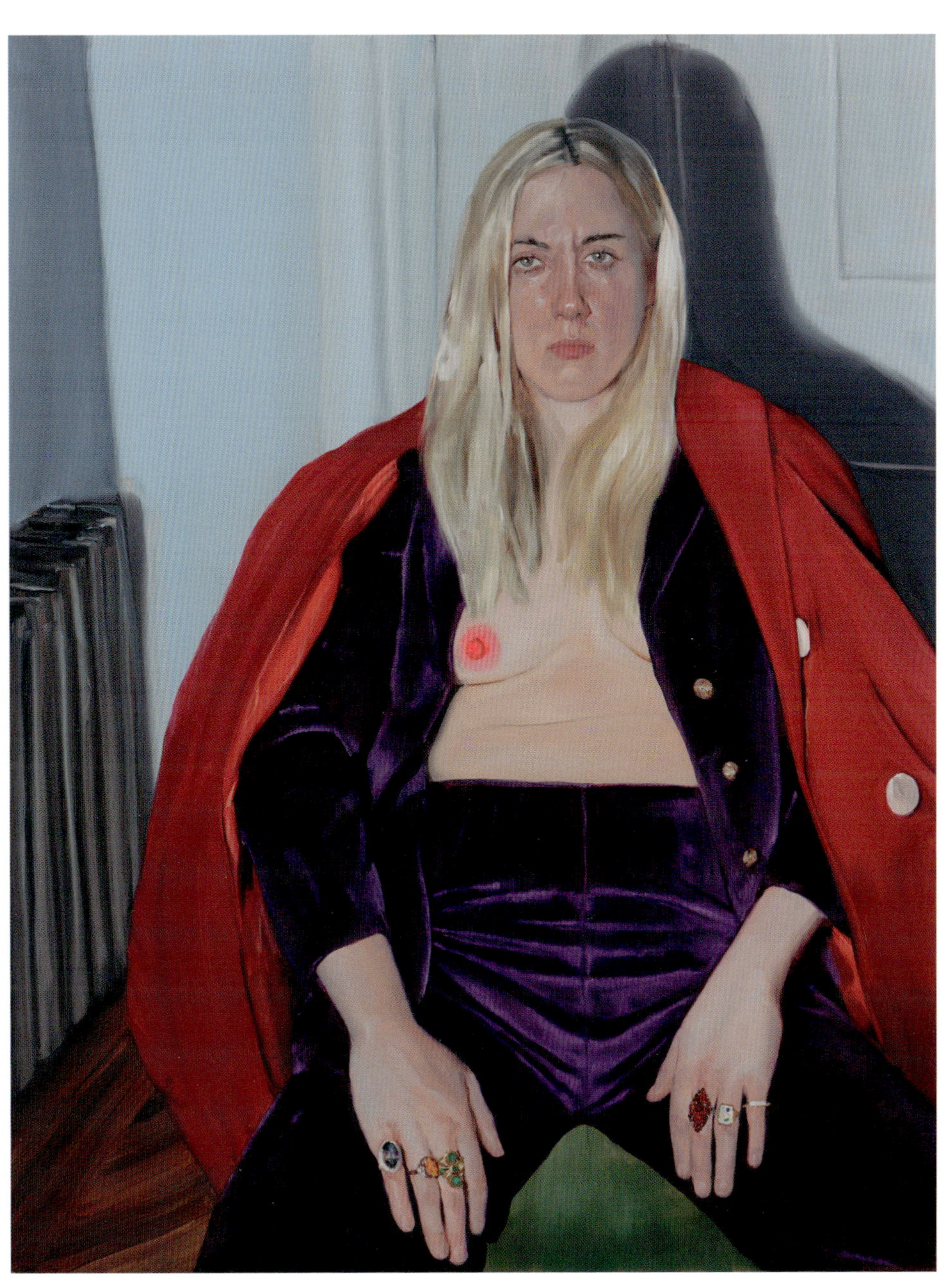

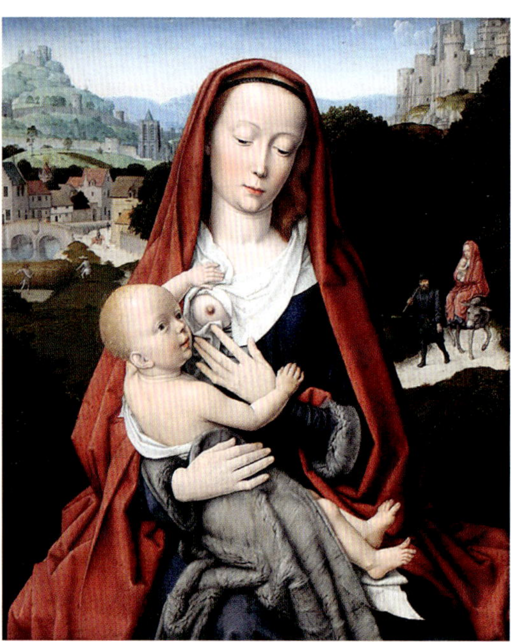

Fig. 9. Gerard David, *Virgin and Child*, 1470–1510. Oil on panel, 16 ⅝ × 14 ½ in. (44.2 × 36.9 cm). Gemäldegalerie, Staatliche Museen zu Berlin

Gribbon presents an excess of velvets in three jewel tones, a plethora of rings, the irreverence of a neon nipple—in contrast to the buttoned-up men painted by Holbein. "I decided to play up these seductive features to the level of camp," Gribbon says, paying tribute to camp as a "cornerstone of the Queer aesthetic." In this regard, Gribbon's exaggeration and humor are a reminder of the instability of symbols, of the shifts in meaning of an object or gesture in different contexts. For example, though they appear as respectable markers of status and wealth in the sixteenth-century *Sir Thomas More*, puffy red velvet sleeves, ornate gold chains, and fur-lined jackets have different associations in twentieth- and twenty-first-century cultures and fashions and for some modern viewers may align with camp and Queer aesthetics. Inspired by Holbein's meticulous attention to detail, Gribbon creates illusions of tactility of flesh, hair, and fabric. Whereas Holbein's extreme fineness in paint application seems to efface the hand of the artist, Gribbon's efficient, broad brushstrokes instead create convincing illusions while leaving evidence of facture, of the hand holding the brush.

The circulation and experience of images through social media—its aesthetics, voyeuristic elements, and the visual relationships between image and text, among other things—informs Gribbon's practice. In contrast to this, the physical setting of Gribbon's work at Frick Madison (the "here" referred to in the painting's title) activates the work. Only here, standing before the painting on the second floor of Frick Madison, adjacent to the sixteenth-century *Thomas Cromwell*, and apprehending Gribbon's title, one is prompted to become aware of oneself and to consider what one is doing in that place. The site of viewing becomes part of the painting's experience. Gribbon continued

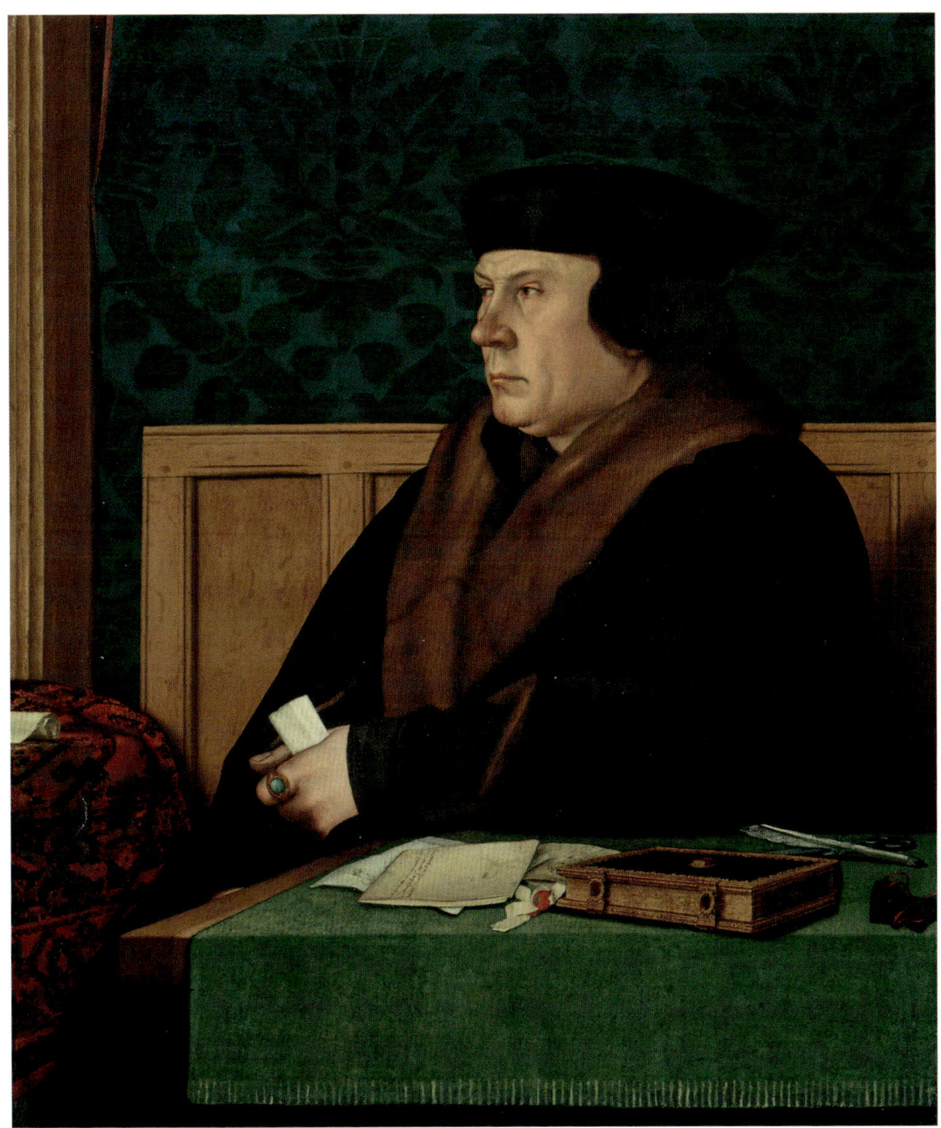

Fig. 10. Hans Holbein the Younger, *Thomas Cromwell*, 1532–33. Oil on oak panel, 30 ¾ × 25 ¼ in. (78.1 × 64.1 cm). The Frick Collection, New York

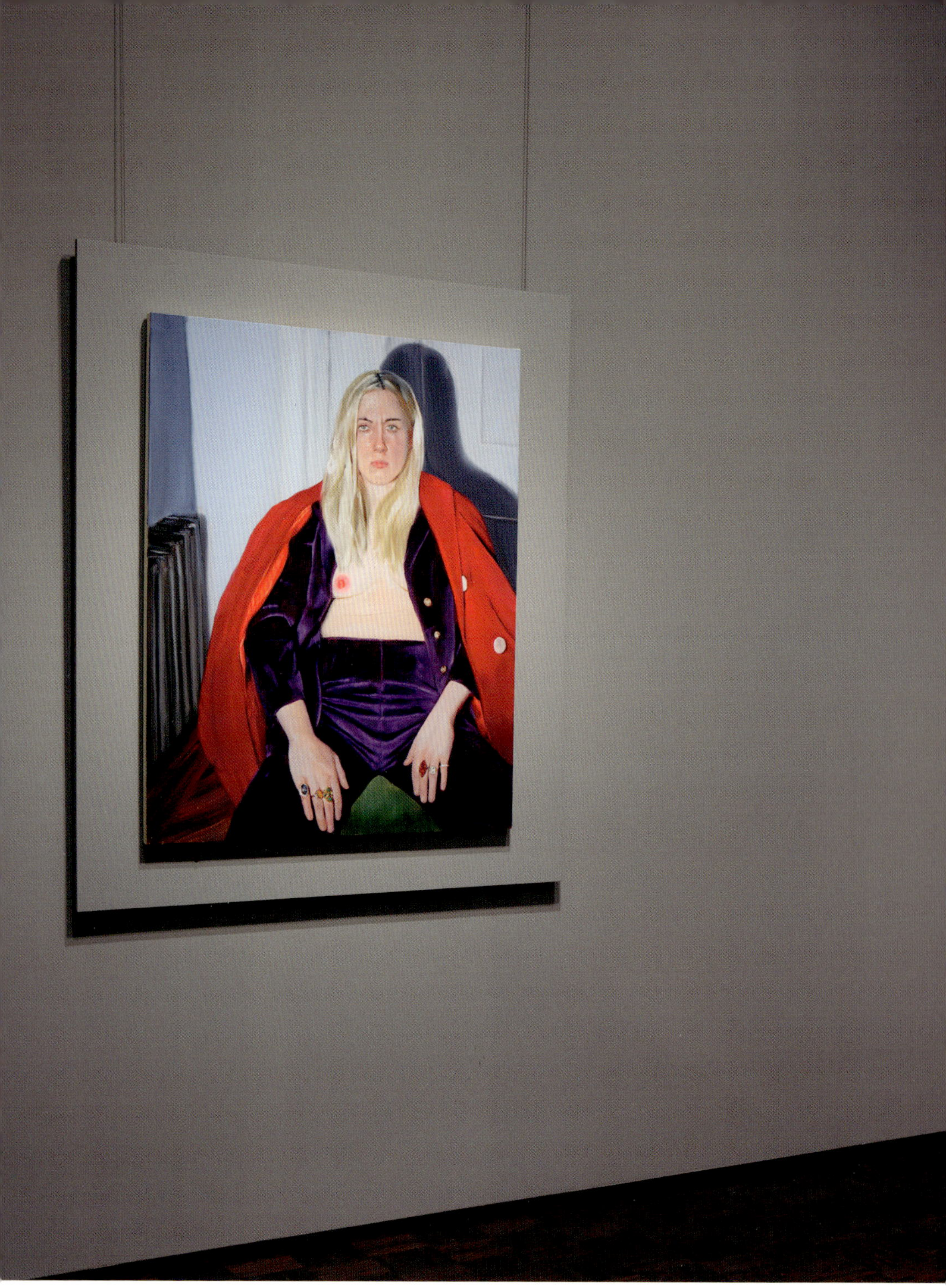

Fig. 11. Installation view of *Living Histories*
Left: Jenna Gribbon, *What Am I Doing Here? I Should Ask You the Same*, 2022 (cat. 1)
Right: Hans Holbein the Younger, *Thomas Cromwell*, 1532–33 (fig. 10)

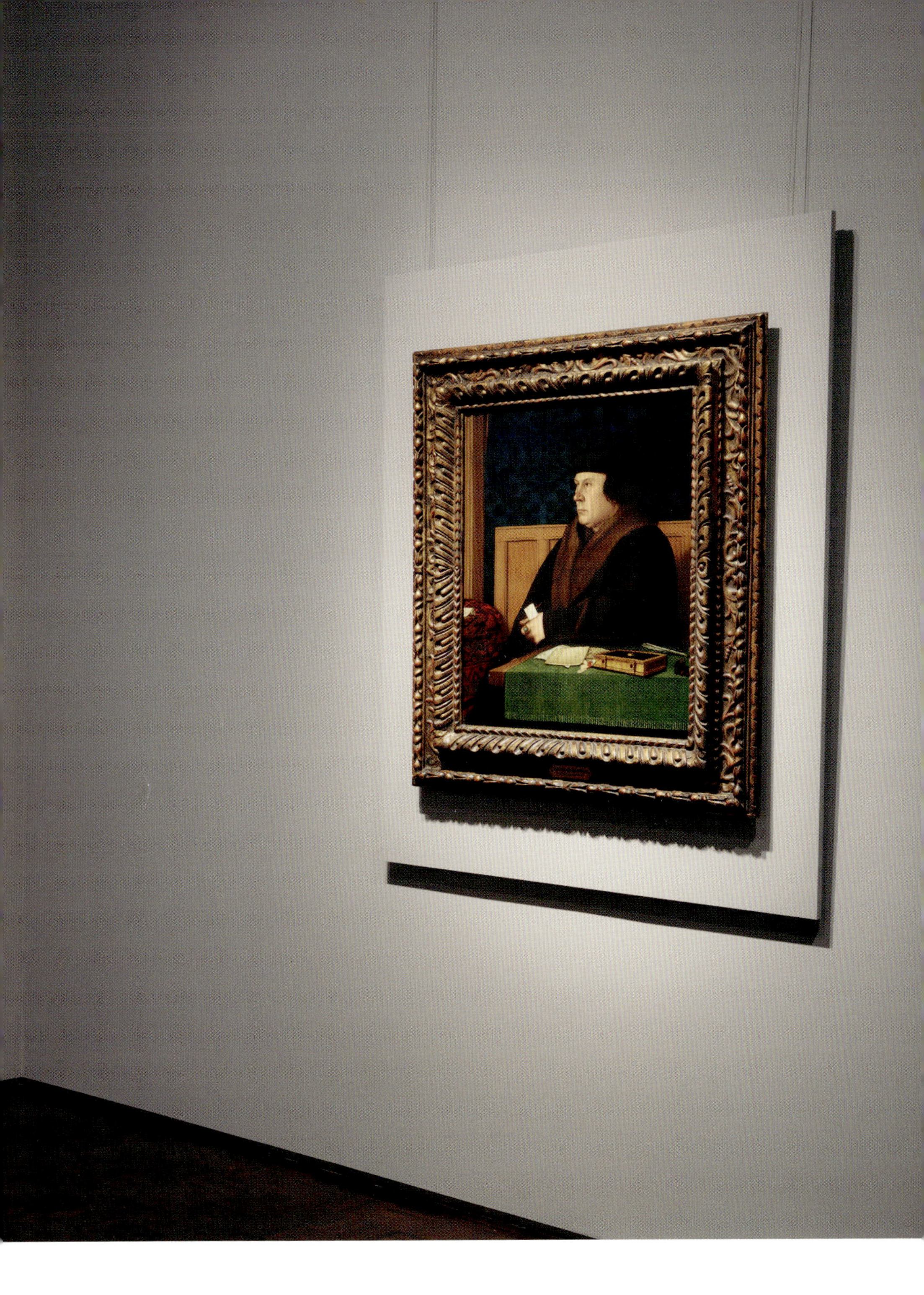

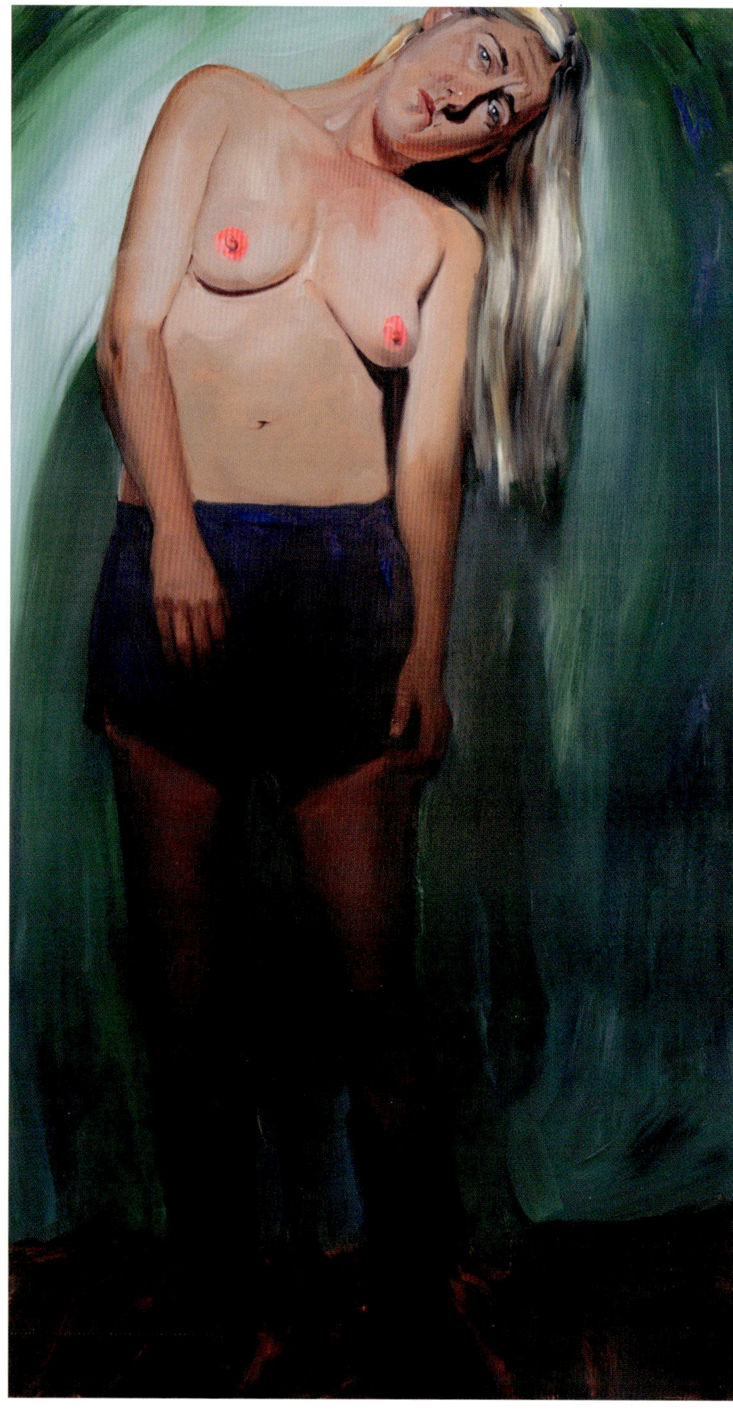

Fig. 12. Jenna Gribbon, *Too Big for the Painting*, 2022. Oil on linen, 80 × 42 in. (203.2 × 106.7 cm). Collection Aishti Foundation, Lebanon

to explore the limits and possibilities of the physical experience of painting in a subsequent 2022 exhibition at the Isaac Bell House in Newport, Rhode Island.[1] Set in a room of a Gilded Age Newport mansion, her *Too Big for the Painting* (fig. 12) presents a topless Mackenzie contorted within the bounds of the painting's edges, a reflection on physicality, on viewers' expectations, and on transgressing the norms of portraiture (these tensions were amplified by its display adjacent to a work by John Currin of a nude woman with enormous, comically inflated breasts).

It is central to the installation of *What Am I Doing Here? I Should Ask You the Same*—both in the context of the meager representation of women artists in collections of European art like the Frick and in the historic context of Holbein, More, Cromwell, and the king they worked for, Henry VIII, whose dispensing of wives has long served as the background of a story about men and power—that the artist and subject are women. Gribbon asserts her subject's presence in ways very different from the demure portraits of women typical in Holbein's time and for centuries later. That artist and subject are Queer women and partners further underscores the painting's tensions with history, denying the dominance of heteronormative power structures and patriarchy. All the while, Gribbon's work remains seductive, its color, forms, and illusions of lush materials and impeccable white flesh pointing to the fraught and enduring tension between conventions of beauty and depictions of women. **AN**

Note

1. Installation view of *Pictus Porrectus: Reconsidering the Full-Length Portrait*, Isaac Bell House, July 1–October 2, 2022.

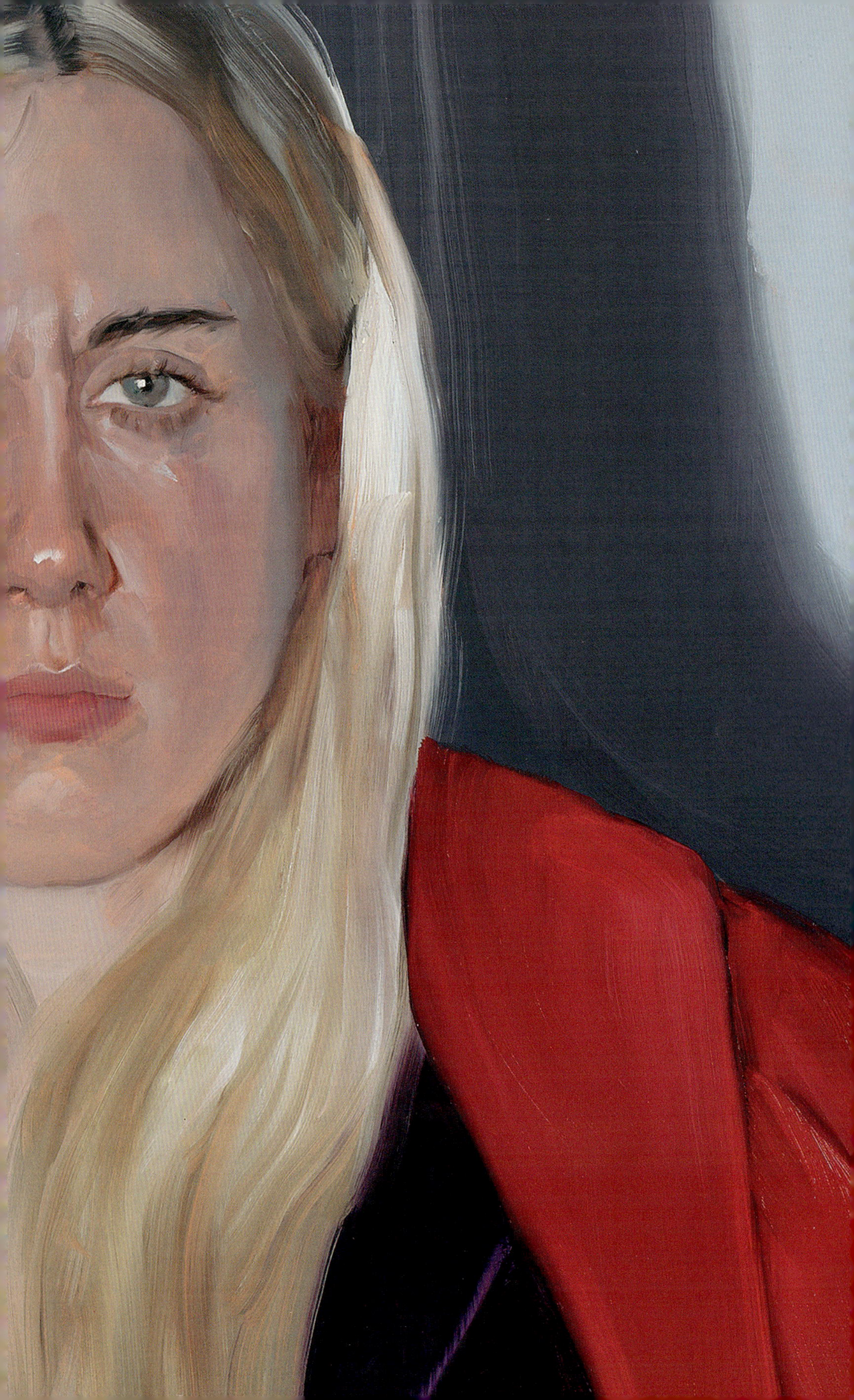

Jenna Gribbon

in Conversation with Legacy Russell

LEGACY RUSSELL — Perhaps the best place to start is with the title of your painting, *What Am I Doing Here? I Should Ask You the Same*. Can you unpack that a bit?

JENNA GRIBBON — The title is meant to be open-ended in that you're not sure if it refers to me or the subject. It kind of refers to both of us because when you see a portrait in a museum, I think one of the first things you think about is who that person is and why they got to be there. My intention was to make the painting a little confrontational in that way and also to put the viewer in a position where they're questioning their usual role in consuming a portrait in a museum and what it means to consume a portrait in a museum. Seeing this Queer woman in this confrontational position with this confrontational expression raises a lot of questions. A lot of questions I wanted to pose came from my own feelings about being included in this space. Museums are really aspirational spaces for me. As a child, I never went to art museums, so I carry with me such gratitude for even getting to enter one, and the idea of exhibiting in one is almost mind-boggling. When I was approached to do this project, it was kind of unbelievable. It triggered a bit of imposter syndrome: "Do I deserve to be in the space? Is this really going to happen?"

While the "I should ask you the same" part of the title is confrontational, it's also an invitation because I really want to ask you the same. I want to ask the viewer, "What are you doing here? And what are your experiences with museums?" Maybe some people have spent their lives going to museums and not really thinking about their role as consumers of art. Maybe it's just an interesting thing to contemplate, and maybe many museum visitors have never been asked to interrogate their own role in this dynamic before.

LR — Growing up in New York, I did go to museums, but I was always very much aware of not being able to see myself in some of these uptown spaces. In entering a place like the Frick, you are hyperaware of the way in which there are so many people in the room but how so few of them, if any, look like you. So, for me, this idea of speaking as a Black woman, as a Queer-identified woman, is really important in the context of the imposter syndrome. Your work being at the Frick is this incredibly decadent, gorgeous, strategic, volatile proposition. It allows the institution to do something different in a way that is nonetheless super historical. And, of course, with the artists who are in the series—Doron and Salman, you and Toyin—this is a really important moment to grapple with

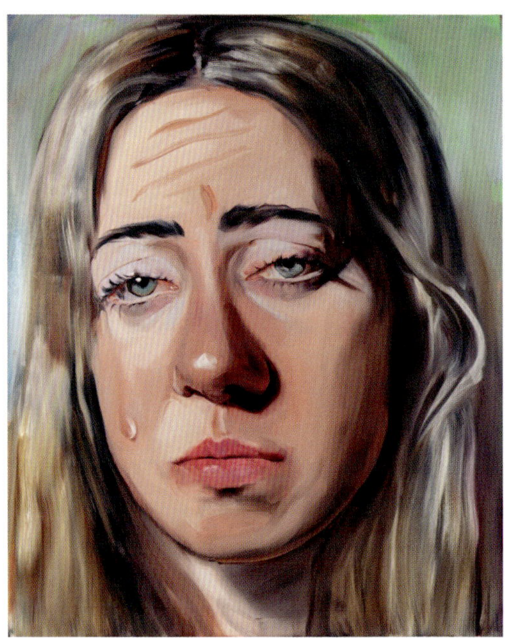

Fig. 13. Jenna Gribbon, *Fake cry*, 2022. Oil on linen, 80 × 64 in. (203 × 162.5 cm). Private collection

the histories of subjecthood, of representation, of Queerness, of visibility. So the presence of your painting does this important, intimate work of bringing folks into this question of "What am I doing here? I should ask you the same." Can you talk a little bit more about what this question means?

JG – There are so many paintings at the Frick that I have looked to over the years and so many artists who are my painting heroes. But it's complicated because there are almost no women in the collection. So I wanted to deal with that but also express how much I love the collection. I wanted to show the reality of that complicated relationship.

I also wanted to embed in the painting a bit of institutional critique—something that doesn't really exist in the core collection. Everyone is very pleased with themselves and not questioning anything. Everyone's like, "Oh, it's great, this world of no women or people of color or Queer people. We're all very happy sitting here with our placid expressions and our nice clothes, and no one is poor." But it's a weird world to walk around in. You walk around at the Frick, and you're like, "What is this reality?" This doesn't reflect any reality I've ever lived in. I'm sure it didn't reflect the reality that these people lived in either.

LR – Even though your painting is in a public space, there's a privacy that is created, almost as a kind of secret, encrypted exchange. That provides an opportunity to ask questions about what it means to participate in being represented and have that be an empowered experience versus something that feels more extractive. What has that felt like, being somebody who is female-identified, who is Queer, doing that act of representation and having that be a participatory exchange that allows for everybody to come to the table in a way that feels equitable.

JG — Choosing my partner as the subject was important (figs. 12–14) because I know her so intimately, and I know how she sees herself, how she likes to be seen. Throughout the process, she can tell me how she feels about things; so it's very collaborative and participatory. The other thing is that my partner is a performer, a musician, and also something of a public figure; so the work ends up being a lot about public versus private. My paintings vacillate between depictions of private moments that are kind of stolen and more about intimacy and others that are more performative, like this one. A lot of times you can tell that I'm working in that performative sphere because I'll use dramatic lighting that's glaring and almost like a spotlight, as opposed to natural light or light that looks convincingly domestic.

LR — You have the sitter posed theatrically in this decadent purple velvet—with her jacket open and a nipple exposed. Everything else in the frame might tell us that this is a real image, but there's something about the hypersaturated colors that brings a deep intensity of character, of eroticism, of fantasy. Seeing your amazing painting at the Frick helps us understand just how staged so many other works are.

JG — Some of the biggest questions of our time are, "What are we looking at? Is it real or is it fake?" The line between fiction and reality is so blurred now. I often like to highlight the artificiality of the painting with this over-the-top, bright, almost theatrical lighting. So even though the sitter is in this domestic setting—in our home—she's in this extremely bright light that makes the clothes brighter. And this theatricality ties it into the Queer aesthetic of camp and theatricality and fantasy, which I wanted to reference. As a Queer person, I find fantasy so important, because in terms of representation—especially lesbian representation—there's so little of it that fantasy is required just to imagine yourself as a part of anything or to be able to see yourself in relation to a fictional character, for example. I enjoy going through the museum and looking at everything through a camp lens because so many of those images are completely over the top. It's a very lighthearted, loving, and humorous way to go through the museum and experience those works. Through my painting, I want to encourage viewers to think about some of the other paintings in that

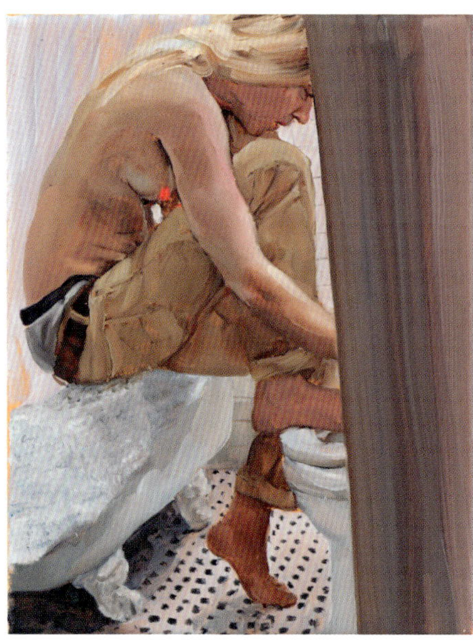

Fig. 14. Jenna Gribbon, *Toe nail trim*, 2021. Oil on linen, 12 × 9 in. (30.5 × 22.9 cm). Private collection

way also, to be like, all this velvet is pretty ridiculous, and all of these jewels are really over the top, and that hat is silly or whatever. Once you look at one painting that way, you can look at them all that way. There's a lot of drama.

LR – This may be a tricky question, but I'm wondering if there is any spiritualism in your painting practice?

JG – Art fills a part of my life much the way religion does for others. Painting is very meditative for me. And, obviously, my partner and I have a very spiritual connection, which I hope comes through in the painting. There's definitely something alchemical about the exchange between her creative force and mine, and I don't think it's an accident that my work ignited in a different kind of way when we began our relationship. But the painting isn't religious in any way that Thomas More would recognize. Another thing that's important in terms of your question is that she's too unashamed to have the religious affiliation that most of the people in that gallery have, which is a mostly Catholic version of religion and full of shame. Most of the women depicted in the Frick's collection are blushing demurely. When I paint women blushing, I want it to be clear they're blushing out of pleasure. Mackenzie's face, though, is almost drained of color. There's nothing coy or demure about her. And she's completely unabashed in her power and her sexuality, in her nakedness. She's very clearly not wearing her hair-shirt.

LR – Yeah, there is no hair-shirt in the image, and More definitely was a fan of the hair-shirt. Something that I've watched grow over time is the celebration of your practice as the images of your work travel online. Can you talk about that?

JG — So much culture in our time takes place on the Internet, and I don't think that's a bad thing. If your work isn't being disseminated in that sphere, then maybe it's not really relevant to what our time is thinking about. So I'm very happy that my work translates well and communicates something to people in that sphere. But I'm a painter who makes these physical objects, so I'm always happy for people to have the experience of engaging with the physical object, seeing the surface of the painting, and feeling the physicality of the paint. The Frick really prioritizes that experience. Going to see a painting at the Frick is like an old-school pilgrimage. That's very different from just scrolling through, coming across the painting, pondering it for a few seconds, and then moving on, and you aren't even allowed to take photos, so you have to be very present and commit the works to memory with only your eyes and bodily experience. I really value the opportunity to have people engage with my work in that really deep, meaningful way that I think is only possible in person.

LR — Can you talk about what painting has given you in the context of these rich traditions, some of which are inside the walls of the Frick and some of which reside beyond them and probably would never enter into that space.

JG — I grew up in a family that didn't have art books, in a part of the country that didn't have many museums. I didn't see any paintings in real life until I was twelve or thirteen. So it was a revelation to discover, through painting, this whole other world that existed outside of my world. It gave me the gift of possibility. It was like if this could exist, then anything is possible, like there's a whole world outside of what I know. And that's so hopeful for a child. That's what painting has given me.

LR — As a last question, what do you imagine as the future of this painting as it goes beyond the walls of the Frick, as it takes on other lives?

JG — The painting is going to the Brant Foundation, where it will pose very different questions. It's so interesting to think about what we want to get out of our experience when we go to a museum and what I, as the artist, want people to walk away with after encountering my work and spending time with it. Thinking about those questions will carry over into all future projects. It's in the work, and it will continue to be.

2

Doron Langberg

Lover

2021
Oil on linen, 30 × 24 in. (76.2 × 70 cm)
High Museum, Atlanta; Promised gift of John Auerbach

Hans Holbein's 1527 portrait of Sir Thomas More was created after the painter had traveled to England for the first time and gotten to know More through a circle of humanist scholars. For part of the two years Holbein spent in London, between the autumn of 1526 and 1528, he may have lived in More's house. The portrait (see fig. 16) is clearly the result of a close relationship and sustained observation of its subject. One can easily imagine how, over the days spent in the home of his patron, Holbein would have observed every angle of his physical appearance: the inquisitive eyes, the tight lips, the grizzled stubble, the fidgeting hands used to handle royal documents. The portrait is an extraordinary essay on reflection. Every texture of More's outfit is delicately and lovingly described: the sheen of the black silk, the thickness of the red velvet, the plushness of the coffee-colored fur. More sits in front of Holbein, lost in thought, his gaze fixed on something in the far distance, his hands grasping a blank letter. He is materially described in every detail yet remains inscrutable.

Similarly, Langberg's *Lover* is rooted in an intimate knowledge of his sitter. The size of the canvas used—an unusual one for Langberg—echoes the dimensions of Holbein's panel. For the first time, Langberg experimented with a larger format, one that directly relates to the painting he was responding to. The crop of the image is tight, as in the Holbein. Very little air is left around the two men, and the background—a green velvet curtain half-drawn in front of a gray wall, or a combination of plush cushions, in different fabrics and colors—is a setting against which the heads of the two men emerge into the pictorial space. For Langberg, it is not important for viewers to know who the sitter in *Lover* is. The artist often represents private body parts or heads in closely cropped compositions (see fig. 18), giving the first name of the sitter or the word *lover* as the title of the paintings. Langberg is interested in the intimacy reflected in the act of portrayal, an intimacy that usually stems from bonds of friendship and love.

The space inhabited by the sitter in *Lover* is as inaccessible as that behind Holbein's *Sir Thomas More*. We can envision a sofa, or a bed, in an otherwise undefined room. The white priming of the canvas, and a liquid rainbow of colors, in the upper left corner, are the only suggestions of a space beyond that on which the artist chooses for us to focus. The man, unlike More, is not described in terms of what his clothes reveal of his status—no fur and velvet, no gold chain of office. For Holbein and for More, the visual representation of the sitter's standing in society was paramount. Langberg's sitter is not portrayed in

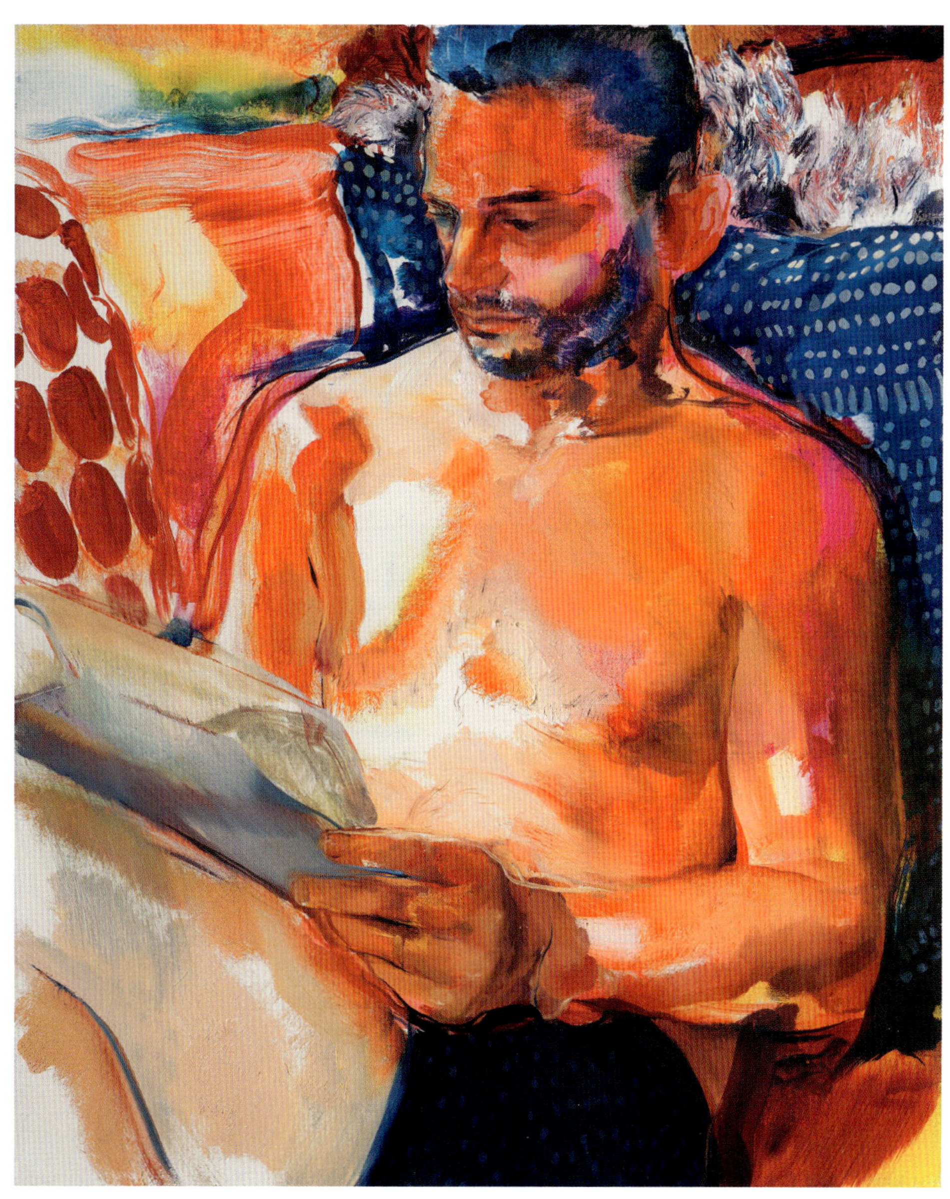

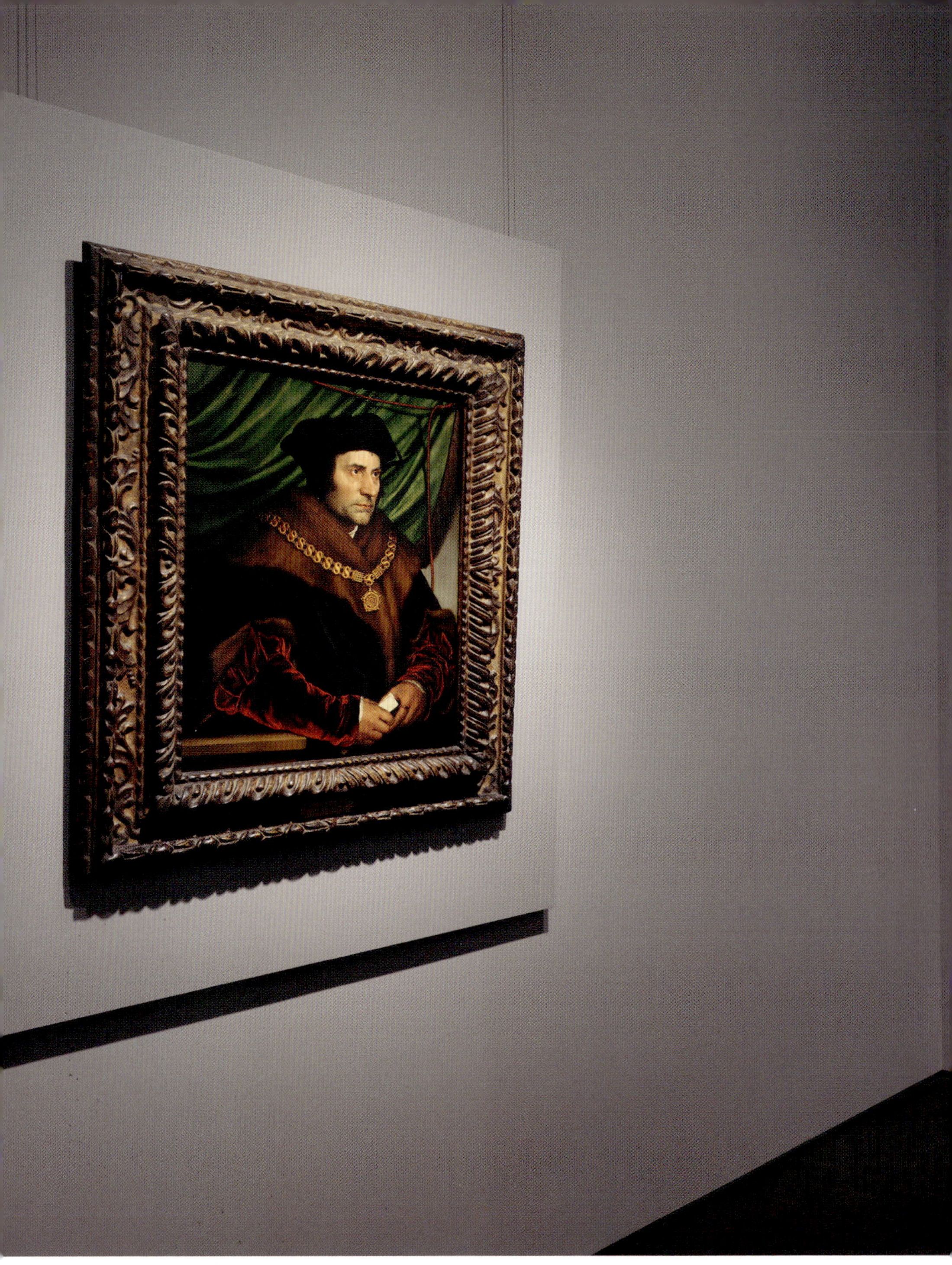

Fig. 15. Installation view of *Living Histories*
Left: Hans Holbein the Younger,
Sir Thomas More, 1527 (fig. 16)
Right: Doron Langberg, *Lover*, 2021 (cat. 2)

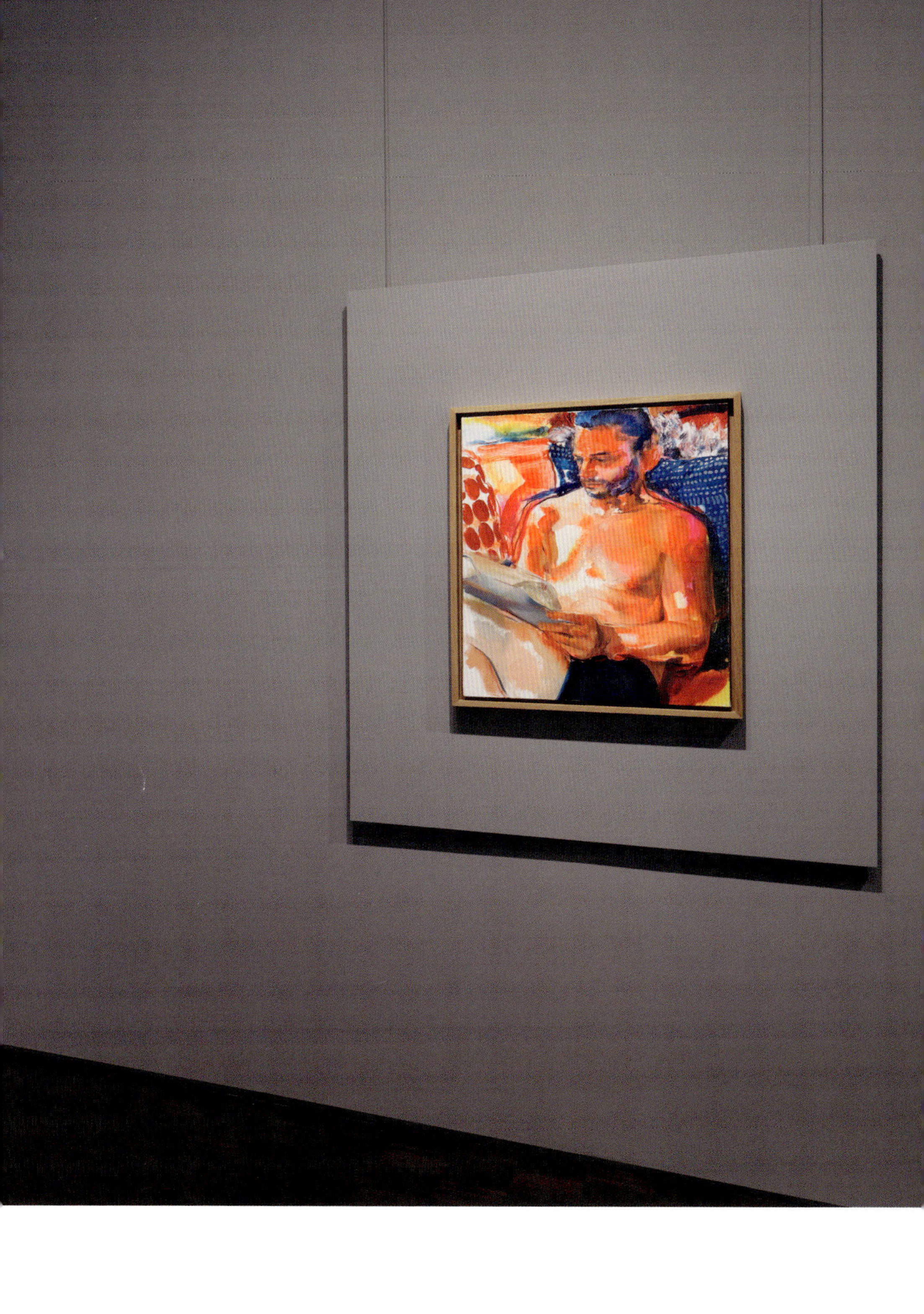

these terms—he is not wearing a lawyer's or businessman's suit, a poet's T-shirt, or a doctor's scrubs. His only item of clothing is a pair of dark blue, polka-dot boxer shorts, which convey the tenderness of this moment: an early morning or a late evening. The body of the sitter is familiarly and lovingly portrayed. The composition is centered on the broad shoulders, the chest and belly, while a graceful line demarcates the sitter's calf from his thigh.

The sitter effortlessly holds a stapled sheaf of papers, folded over itself. The viewer, however, is not allowed to know the contents of these documents. The sitter is engrossed in the act of reading, his head slightly tilted, his gaze resolutely fixed on the sheets. While More is lost in thought, staring off into the distance, the figure in *Lover* is absorbed in the papers at hand. Langberg's action of painting does not interrupt him. The tenderness of the artist's observation is remarkable, but we are entering a world that we have not necessarily been invited into. The head of the sitter emerges from the ocean of cushions, a fringe suggesting waves repeatedly crashing on a beach. The

Fig. 16. Hans Holbein the Younger, *Sir Thomas More*, 1527. Oil on oak panel, 29 ½ × 23 ¾ in. (74.9 × 60.3 cm). The Frick Collection, New York

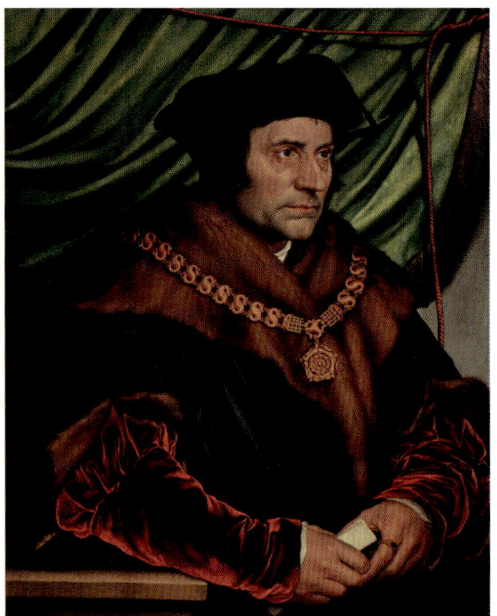

Fig. 17. Gustave Caillebotte, *Portrait of a Man,* 1880. Oil on canvas, 32 × 25 13⁄16 in. (81.3 × 65.6 cm). The Cleveland Museum of Art; Bequest of Muriel Butkin

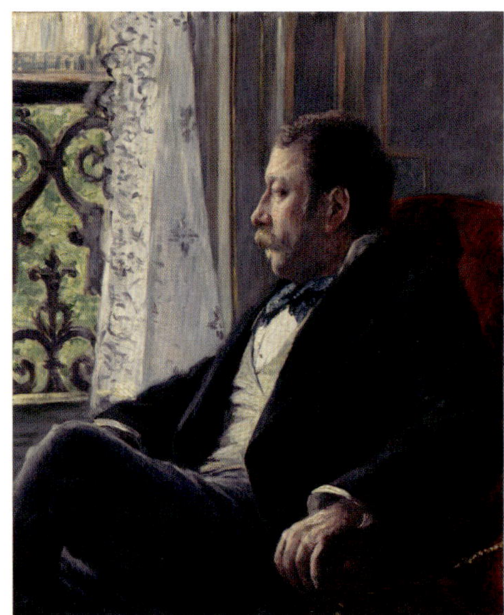

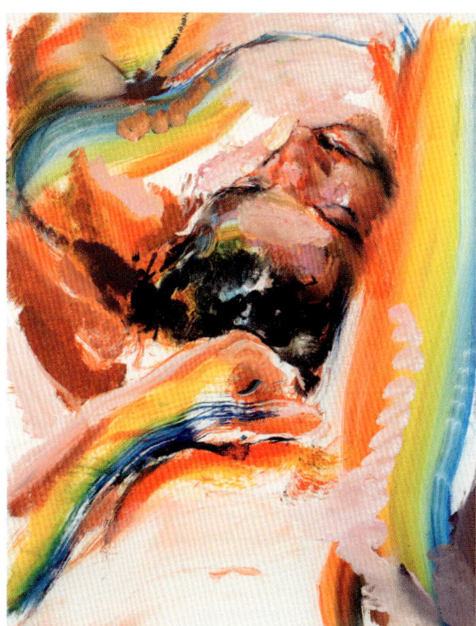

Fig. 18. Doron Langberg, *In My Lap 1*, 2020. Oil on canvas, 24 × 18 in. (60.9 × 45.7 cm). Private collection

blazing, painterly background sets the head of the sitter in sharp focus. The indigo blue of the large cushion—a color cherished by Holbein—spreads to the man's hair and beard. The color reappears, in a darker hue—like a Wagnerian leitmotif—in the sitter's boxer shorts. The man's left hand prominently projects into the viewer's space, pushing beyond the planar surface of the canvas. It is a stylish hand, gently resting on the thigh and propping up the papers for viewing. The identity of the sitter is a secret that the artist—and sitter—keep for themselves. There is one clue, however, to the place the sitter holds in the artist's life. A simple gold ring on the fourth finger of the left hand defines him as a husband.

The impenetrability of Langberg's *Lover* not only answers directly to Holbein's *Sir Thomas More* but resonates with a nineteenth-century tradition of portraiture that was the norm among painters such as Édouard Manet. Langberg's work has often been compared to that of Pierre Bonnard, a painter whose intimate portrayals of his wife and audacious choices of color have affinities with Langberg. No matter how many times Bonnard lovingly represents his wife Marthe in her bathtub, it is a space that we are barred from entering and that perhaps the painter himself has only had fleeting permission to witness. Like Bonnard, Langberg is a painter of stolen moments, of intimate sparkles. Unlike Holbein, he does not set out to immortalize his figures. Instead, he captures the quotidian moments that life is actually made of. In this respect, Langberg can also be associated with a painter who deserves a place in the pantheon of Queer painting in nineteenth-century France: Gustave Caillebotte. Caillebotte's sitters (fig. 17) are also anonymous men, tenderly and familiarly captured. Their identities remain a source of speculation, but the title *Lover* could be applied to them as well. XS

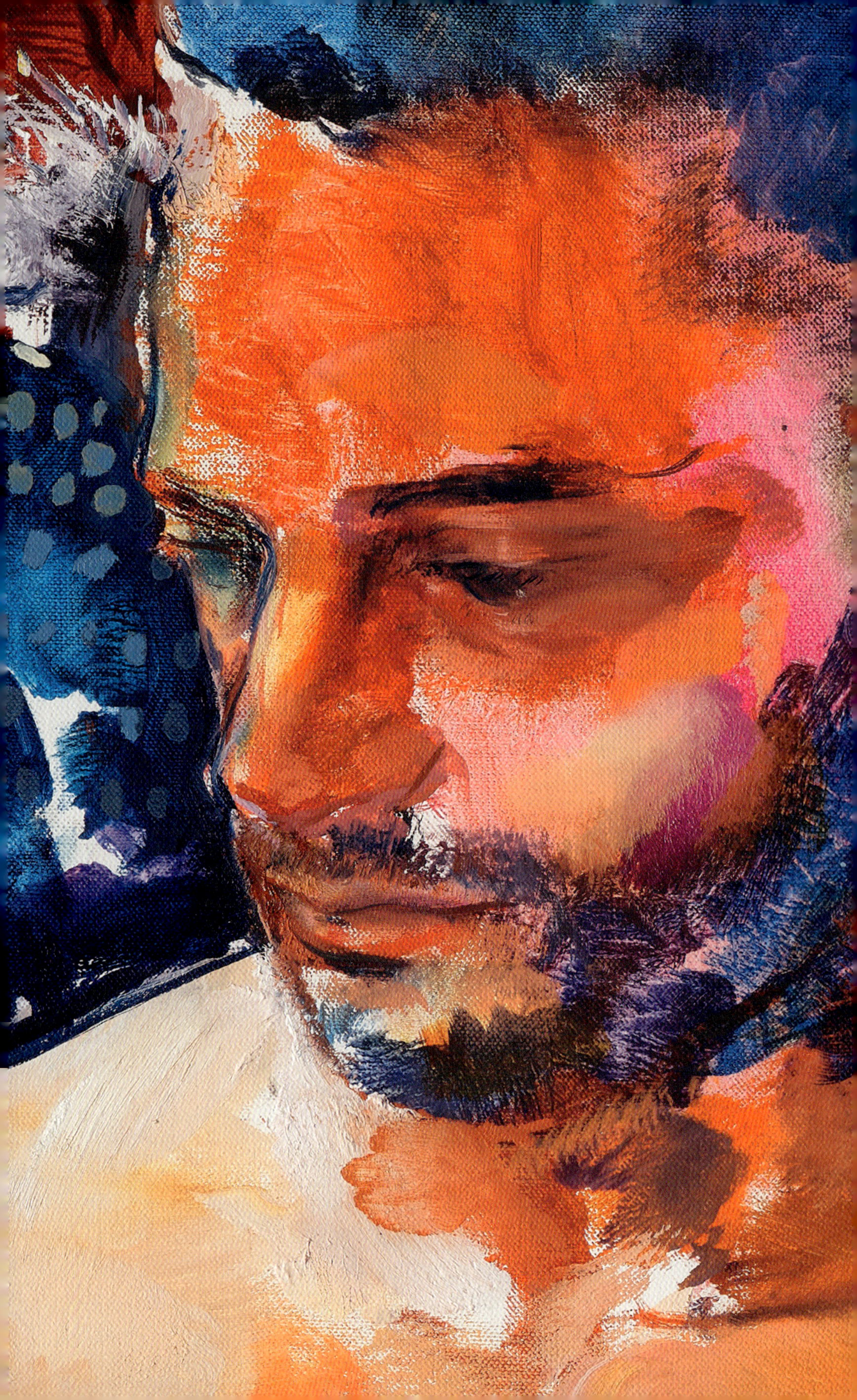

Doron Langberg

in Conversation with Jonathan Anderson

JONATHAN ANDERSON — Let's start at the beginning. The Frick approaches you to do a project. Tell me how that felt.

DORON LANGBERG — I remember getting a text from Xavier Salomon, who put the project together with Aimee Ng, saying can we chat about something? When Xavier proposed the idea, it was a total surprise and a dream-come-true moment. The Frick has never done anything like this before, so it wasn't something that was even imaginable for me. It felt like someone giving me the best gift.

JA – And then you chose to be paired with Holbein? He's one of my all-time favorite painters. As a child, I remember seeing *A Lady with a Squirrel and a Starling (Anne Lovell?)* (fig. 19) at the National Gallery in London and being completely mesmerized. It felt so contemporary and still does. What I'd like to know is why Doron and Holbein?

DL – Actually, Xavier and Aimee assigned the artists to us, but I definitely would have chosen Holbein (see fig. 16). I've been looking at Holbein most of my life, as many painters do, especially those interested in figuration and portraiture. My relationship with him started through his drawings. I was blown away by the refinement of the details and his collage sensibility, where every element of the drawing—the garment, the features, the hair, etc.—is not only described differently but often made using different media. It really shows his keen attention to the tactility of what he's describing, which is something I think a lot about in my paintings.

JA – Holbein seems like one of the first artists to really show a subject warts and all. You feel like the person is present. The National Gallery has recently rehung some galleries, and it was kind of weird seeing Holbein mixed in with things from maybe a hundred years later and seeing how advanced he was.

But anyway, something you mentioned when we talked last week really stuck with me—the idea of friendship and collaboration. That really resonates in my own work and in my relationship to you. I see a wonderful painting of yours that has two men in it—who are friends of yours—and then I become curious as to who they are, and it turns out that they are Joe McShea and Edgar Mosa, who made the set for the Loewe show, which was a couple of weeks ago. It seems that especially in America right now there's an amazing kind of circle of friendship and collaboration. What are your thoughts on that?

DL — I totally think that as well! Your collaboration with Joe and Edgar is an amazing example of that. I met them on Fire Island, walking along the beach on my way to draw at the Meat Rack. They put up these stunning ribbon flags, and I had my tote bag full of drawing supplies, and we were just so intrigued by each other. The following year, they invited me to stay in their share, and I painted them (fig. 20). Russell Tovey, whom we both know and love, put that painting in his show *Breakfast Under the Tree* in Margate, which is how we got connected; and through that, you saw Joe and Edgar's amazing installations and invited them to do your show. These relationships with other Queer artists have been transformative for me and my work these past few years. To a large degree, this Frick project is a reflection of real-world friendships with Salman, Jenna, and Xavier and our mutual admiration of each other's practices.

JA — I've been thinking about different movements in Queer art and of artists like Paul Cadmus and George Platt Lynes, two completely different types,

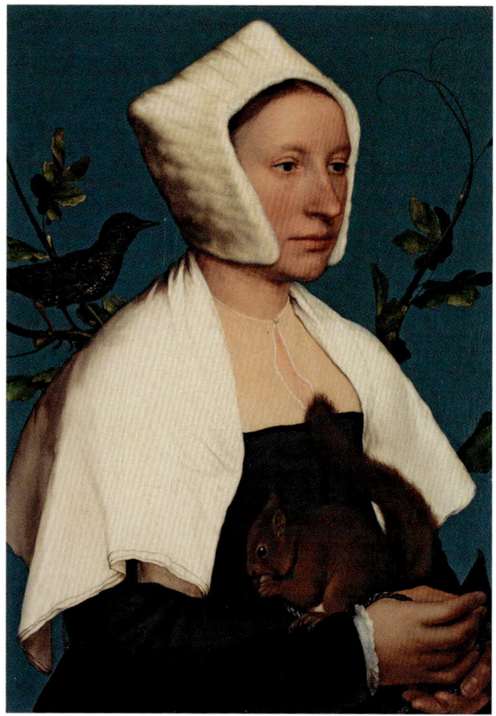

Fig. 19. Hans Holbein the Younger, *A Lady with a Squirrel and a Starling (Anne Lovell?)*, ca. 1526–28. Oil on oak panel, 22 1/16 × 15 1/4 in. (56 × 38.8 cm). The National Gallery, London; Bought with contributions from the National Heritage Memorial Fund and the Art Fund and Mr. J. Paul Getty Jr. (through the American Friends of the National Gallery, London), 1992

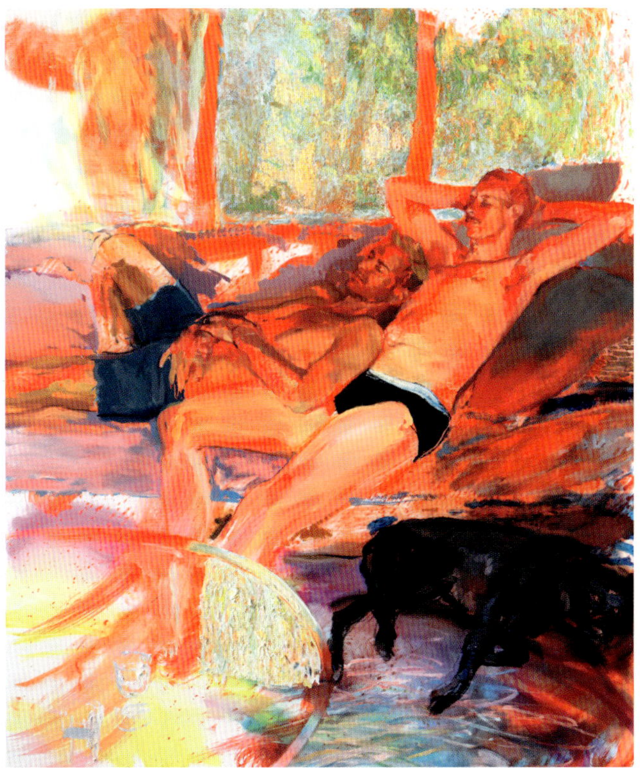

Fig. 20. Doron Langberg, *Joe and Edgar*, 2020. Oil on canvas, 96 × 80 in. (243.8 × 203.2 cm). Private collection

and their depictions of the body. I was thinking of this network of different people who went to Fire Island or were painting on Fire Island or doing needlepoint in that moment. There was this idea of cross-pollination through collaborative works.

And then poof—we wind forward to this period, and it's completely different. You have popular media, social media. Queer culture has become this volcano that has erupted, landed, and sort of solidified. Within the process of making Queer art today, what is that experience for you now? How does it make you feel? Is it about being on the outskirts, or is it about being in the middle of it, or is it a bit of both?

DL – From my perspective, the visibility of Queer art definitely feels more central and public right now. It's fascinating to consider the present moment in relation to the artists you mentioned. It makes me think of the show *The Young and Evil*, brilliantly curated by my friend Jarrett Earnest in 2019 at David Zwirner, which chronicled the work of the PaJaMa collective and that generation of artists. It was very meaningful to see how their friendship was integral to their work. Some of the pieces in the show that were more explicitly Queer or sexual, they made for each other as this private practice that is only intended for themselves. Looking at these pieces decades later, they feel so familiar and relevant. For Queer artists, and Queer people, there's a necessity and desire to stick together in order to live our lives and make our work. Fire Island, being this separatist Queer utopia, is the ultimate manifestation of that. You really see how generative that community was over the decades—with artists like Paul Thek, Frank O'Hara, Edmund White, and David Hockney—and how generative it is today, with so many Queer artists hanging out and making work there.

JA — It's interesting that you mention Paul Thek, who is one of my heroes—an artist well before his time. I've only ever read or looked at works of Fire Island—never actually been there—but in a weird way, when you look at those amazing Fire Island pictures by Peter Hujar, you realize that with a liberal community designed for community, there's this idea of flexibility within it. You get this sense of collaboration, of network, this incredible sense of letting go. When creatives talk to one another, it can only help fuel more creativity. It's one of these amazing things that should be done in giant forums.

We see some of these links—between Thek and Hujar, for instance—only in hindsight. But we do have transparency today and this idea of the voice of the artists. A viewer can become quite submerged. When I follow you on Instagram or in the press, I feel like I'm following the journey of someone, the evolution of your work. I actually saw your work for the first time in the flesh in Margate, and I realized that while the Internet is great, it only goes so far. And seeing your work in the flesh I realized that it is not as simple as it might look. This is a good point to segue into the process of painting. How do you build up your central character, your landscape?

DL — The starting point of my work is my personal relationship with my subject, which is always someone I know, whether a friend, a partner, or a family member. My feelings toward and knowledge of them is a palpable part of the process—a material, like paint. With a smaller piece like *Lover*, I work from observation, which allows me to gauge, almost brushstroke by brushstroke, if the painting is true to my idea of the person. In addition to seeking out likeness, in these observational sessions I'm looking for ideas about color and materiality that could capture the moment or feeling I'm after. With the Frick project, I also wanted to create a concrete connection to Holbein and the presence of his figures: his unmatched ability to capture texture and detail, the "warts and all" as you were saying before, gives his figures their gravity and power. In my painting, materiality and tactility are expressed through gesture and touch rather than rendering and are used to express the subject's interiority rather than their role in the world.

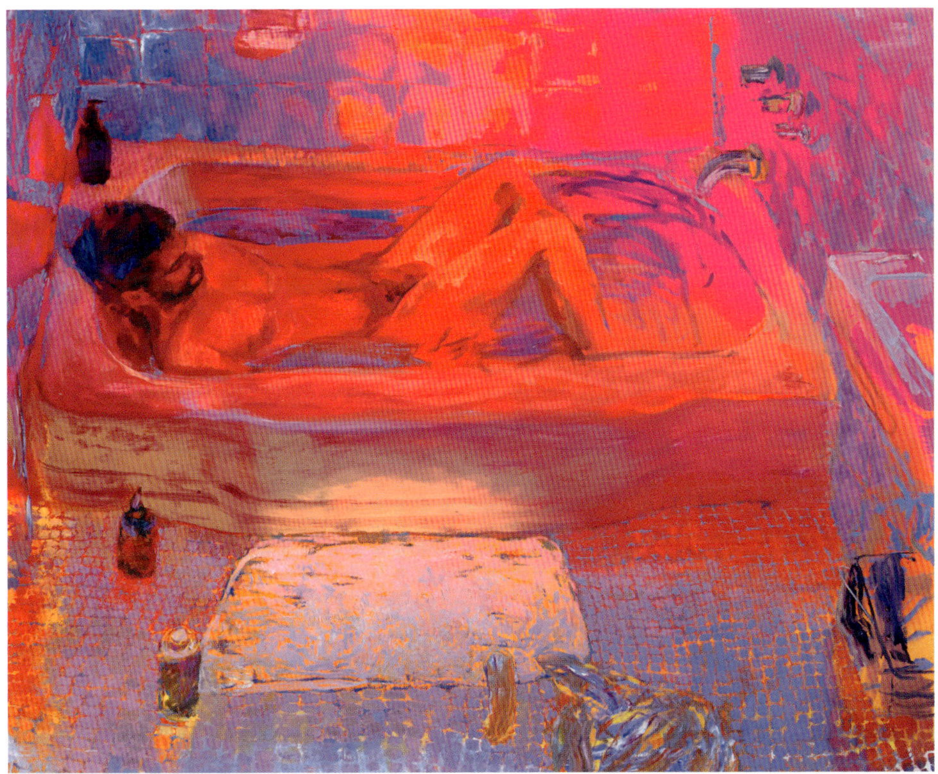

Fig. 21. Doron Langberg, *Bather*, 2021. Oil on canvas, 80 × 96 in. (203.2 × 243.8 cm). Institute of Contemporary Art, Boston

JA — Your portraits are never static. It's as if when you are working on a painting, you kind of rotate around it. And I get the feeling that the subject is there in a kind of cerebral sense as well. The painting really envelops you, whereas with Holbein there's a kind of static likeness, nearly an emotional likeness. It feels like it's alive, sort of coming toward you, which is remarkable.

I'm looking at your picture now and thinking about where landscape becomes body, where body becomes landscape, this idea of how you blend people together. And in a weird way, even this idea of love—whether love of a niece or a partner or friends, there is something incredibly tender. I've always thought the depiction of love is one of the most important things in painting.

DL — I'm so happy you see that in my work. Ultimately, all my paintings are about love. The thing that's most important to me are the people in my life and the relationships that sustain me every day, which give meaning to everything around me (fig. 21). That happens in the studio too—having friends over and talking about painting gives meaning to the process of painting. Having a partner to share so much with deepens my capacity to relate to other people, and also to myself. In my paintings, I try to give form to the different aspects of these relationships—whether joyous and ecstatic or somber and mournful.

JA – There's so much rapid mark-making in your work. This sort of goes back to this idea of movement, this more guttural sense of emotional paint.

Sometimes when I finish a collection, I'm so completely drained. You give birth to this collection, you put it down the runway, and then the minute that every model comes back and you finish the PR process, you can barely talk. It's almost like an incredible rejection process. Do you ever finish a work and feel drained in that way?

DL – Totally! As a medium, painting is not forgiving; it doesn't lie. You can paint over things, you can erase, but the trace remains within the painting, so the stakes are high. A bad painting day can be very hard, so there are a lot of emotional ups and downs in the painting process. There's a rhythm to it where a painting starts with a lot of promise and energy and then it becomes evident that the initial idea was not enough to carry me through the whole process, and I need to rediscover what the painting is about and it gets messy. Finding that clarity is the hardest part and can take weeks. But once I turn a corner and two or three elements in the painting fall into place, it comes together quite fast. And after it's done, I'm ready for it to leave the studio, kind of like that post-show feeling you're describing.

JA – I was going to ask something broader—do you feel that as a Queer painter you have a responsibility somehow?

DL – That's something I've been thinking about since starting to work with Queer subject matter. On the one hand, it's so personal, and I don't want to speak for other people, but on the other, my experiences and my identity are part of a broader social and historical context I cannot ignore. The Frick project was the first time my work was exposed to a general audience. On Instagram, for example, there were a lot of supportive responses but also less supportive ones. I got the sense that people felt they owned the history of painting and that the inclusion of Queer artists in that conversation was somehow insulting to them. This response, which felt unwarranted for such a tame subject—a man with his shirt off—affirmed an idea that is fundamental to my work, that Queerness is not just about the sexual but is all-encompassing, present in every aspect of our lives. Seeing this play out was disheartening but also reassured me that what I'm doing is meaningful.

JA – When social media started to become paramount in marketing, it really affected me. I would read every single thing. Now I really enjoy it—I just find it fascinating when someone dislikes something, when my work creates a kickback. That's what I was getting at when I asked about responsibility. I sometimes feel like I have a responsibility to keep slowly edging that barometer forward because I feel that, in other art forms, it has gone so much further. Sometimes in fashion, you feel like you're slightly bound by the idea of "we have to appeal to everyone." But what is really exciting is not appealing to everyone. It's about questioning things. And yes, sometimes when you have the institution and this idea of breaking up, that's where this idea of Holbein and Doron Langberg on the wall together, this collaborative exchange, can become quite fiery to people. I think this is sort of because you have the classicist and the modernist. But ultimately, Holbein was a modernist who then became a classicist. So maybe what you're doing now will push the barometer forward again, and then in four hundred years we'll look back and be like, how classic Doron is. And this is why this project is so exciting—ultimately because it makes us look at Holbein. A lot of young people may not know who Holbein is, but this Frick project helps break down boundaries between past, present, and future, of where things can go.

DL – Absolutely. This breaking down of boundaries was Aimee and Xavier's curatorial conceit. Even the title of the show, *Living Histories*, suggests that for us, for painters, the paintings in the Frick are artworks that we're responding to as much as we're responding to the work of our peers.

3

Salman Toor

Museum Boys

2021
Oil on panel, 30 × 40 in. (76.2 × 101.6 cm)
Private collection

A series of bright lights—almost a constellation of stars—brings the set out of darkness for the viewer. The light at upper right could be a stage light or a lamp used to illuminate art in an exhibition. The space is colored in a vivid emerald green—a signature hue in the work of Salman Toor—and is undefined, with the exception of a clutter of artworks from different geographical locations and periods, all placed on stone pedestals and columns: Greek and Roman statues and a bust (male figures, presumably depicting mythological loves or an ancient emperor), an Islamic stone slab from a cemetery, a Hindu lingam stone. In the midst of these are a pile of black plastic garbage bags and a round mirror. The mirror is dark and faces the viewer, bringing to mind these lines from Shakespeare's sonnet 77:

> Thy glass will show thee how thy beauties wear,
> Thy dial how thy precious minutes waste;
> . . .
> The wrinkles which thy glass will truly show
> Of mouthed graves will give thee memory;
> Thou by thy dial's shady stealth mayst know
> Time's thievish progress to eternity.

On the floor is a large, patterned rug in the dark red typical of Mughal imperial models. The lingam is the only object between the museum artworks and the central vitrine. The setting suggests a museum, either a specialized one like the Frick, with its Renaissance bronzes and Persian and Indian carpets, or a more encyclopedic one. The disquiet around the holdings of such museums—safe havens for ancient artifacts all too often acquired through colonial plunder—is implied by the selection. Two young men of different skin color meet in the space delineated by the rug. Both are dressed in a haphazard manner: a vest and rags over their upper bodies. A solitary white sneaker is on the foot of the boy on the right. Some items of seventeenth-century clothing have migrated from Vermeer's paintings into this scene: a millstone collar, a pearl earring, and a large-brimmed, black, feathered hat. The boy on the left holds his hands behind his back, echoing the classical pose of the Farnese Hercules. The exposed body parts—the buoyant butt, the hairy legs, and the uncovered penis—are common sights in both painting and statuary in museums, but here they endow the figures with an erotic potential. The boys are encountering works of art and each other in a museum setting.

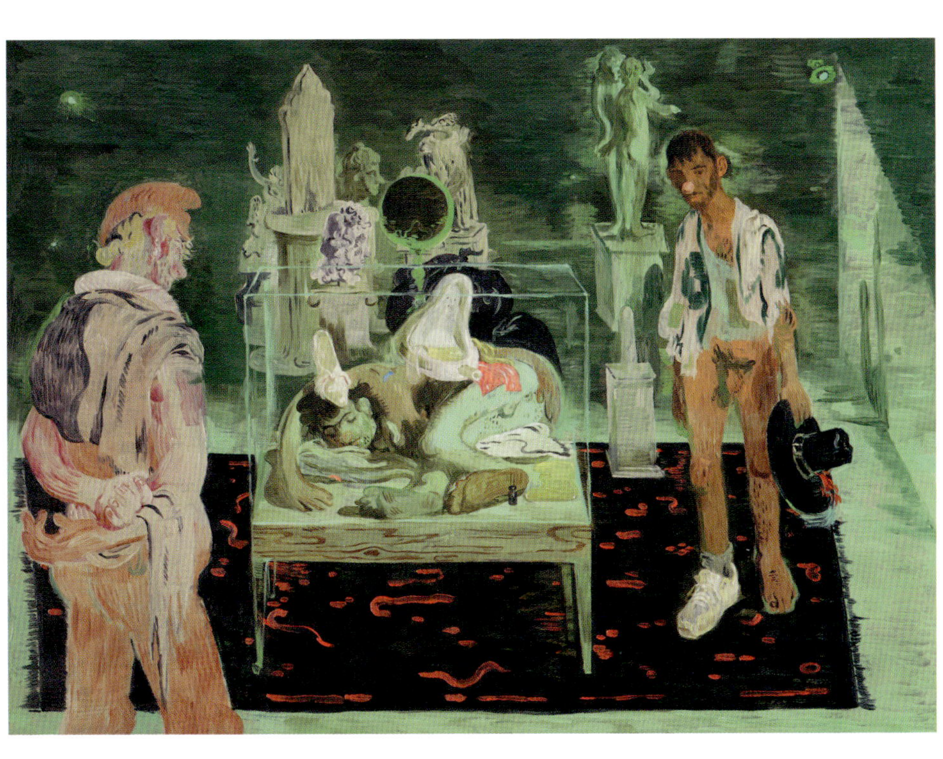

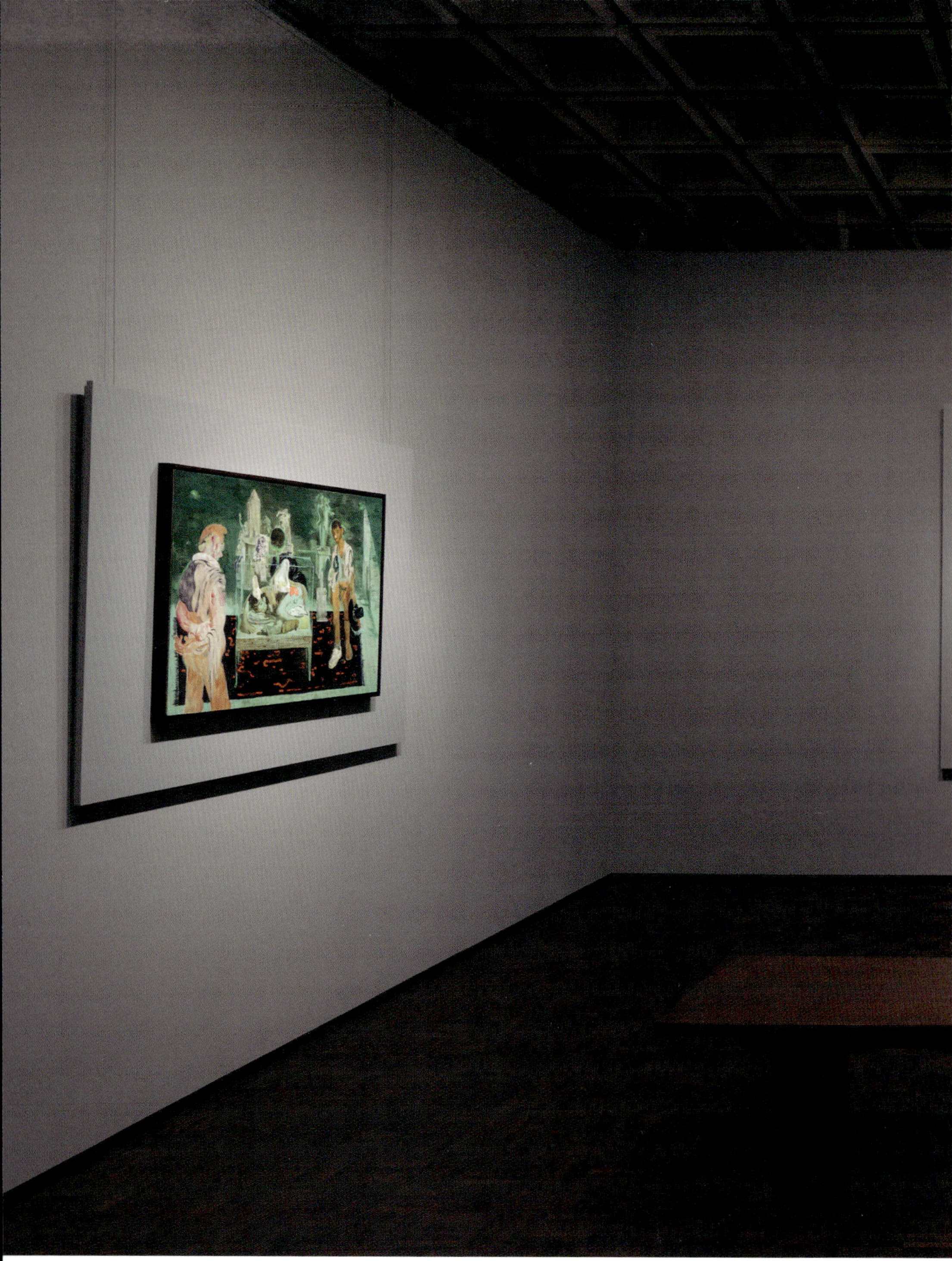

Fig. 22. Installation view of *Living Histories*
Left: Salman Toor, *Museum Boys*, 2021 (cat. 3)
Center: Johannes Vermeer, *Mistress and Maid*, 1666–67. Oil on canvas, 35 ½ × 31 in. (90.2 × 78.7 cm). The Frick Collection, New York
Right: Johannes Vermeer, *Officer and Laughing Girl*, ca. 1657 (fig. 24)

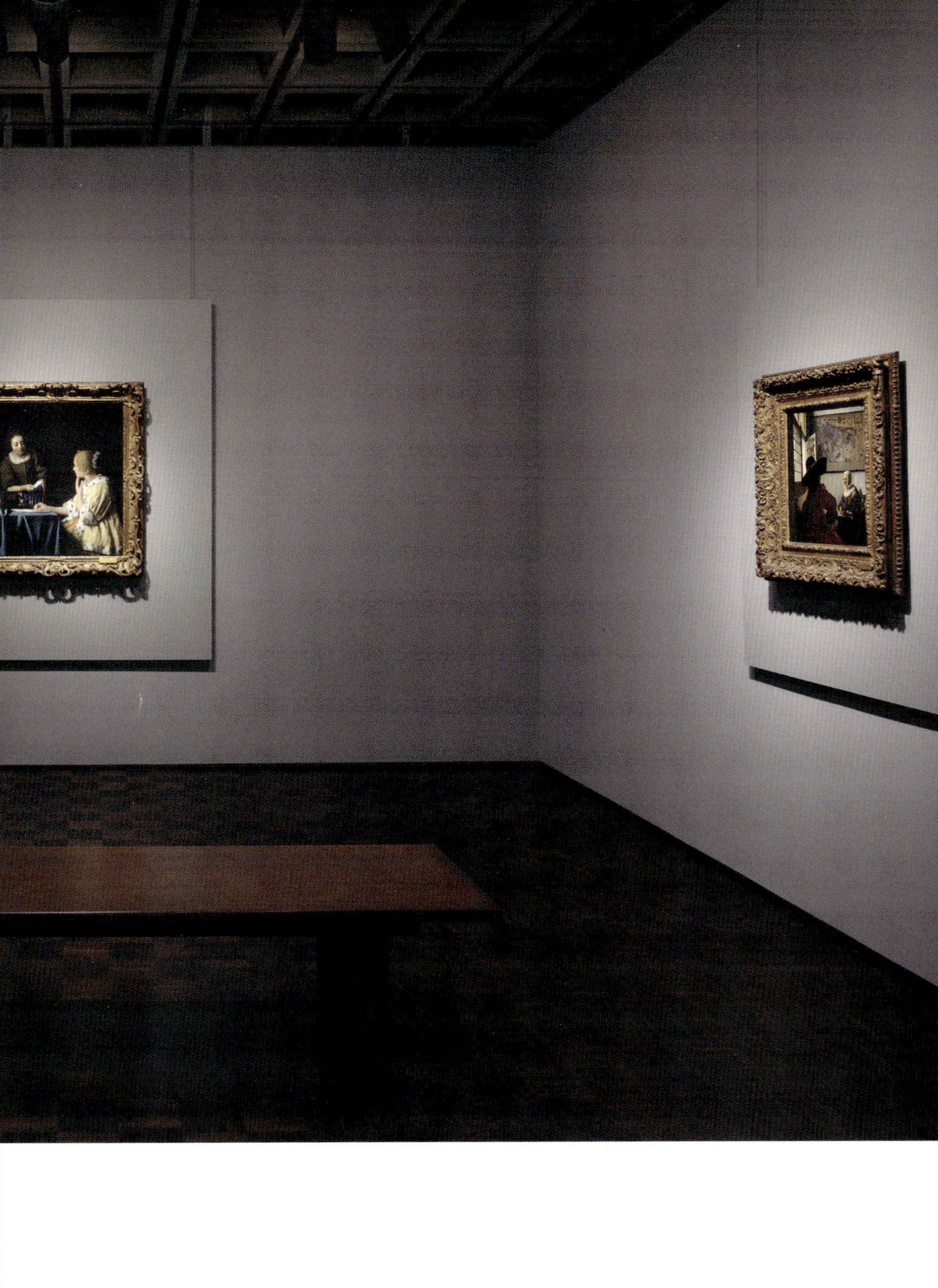

Their gazes, however, are fixed not on each other but on the central feature in the painting.

The vitrine—a more modern artifact compared to the classicizing plinths in the background—contains two nude male bodies, wearied by physical activities easily imagined. Their forms are intertwined in an intricate knot, one of the boy's arms embracing the other form as they lie close to a body of spilled liquid. Around them is a still life of objects: a urinal, rags, a small bottle, a prophylactic, and a woman's shoe.

Toor's work always encourages close looking and interpretation (fig. 23). It urges the acceptance of a mood and a feeling, embracing what is before our eyes and letting our imaginations connect the dots. The relationship between the boys in the vitrine and those outside it is enigmatic. Is it a co-existence of present and past or a premonition of things to come? Toor's work has been related to the tradition of Mughal miniatures in the northern Indian subcontinent. A work such as *The Mughal Emperor Shah Jahan with His Ancestor Timur* (fig. 25) depicts the impossible encounter between the emperor and his distant forebear—spanning almost two centuries in time. Museums are sites of convergence between different times and cultures, where the present

Fig. 23. Salman Toor, *Four Friends*, 2019. Oil on panel, 40 × 40 in. (101.6 × 101.6 cm). Private collection

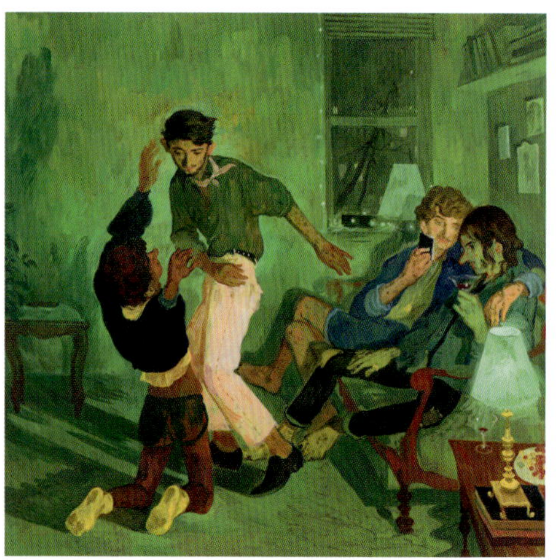

Fig. 24. Johannes Vermeer, *Officer and Laughing Girl*, ca. 1657. Oil on canvas, 19 ⅞ × 18 ⅛ in. (50.5 × 46 cm). The Frick Collection, New York

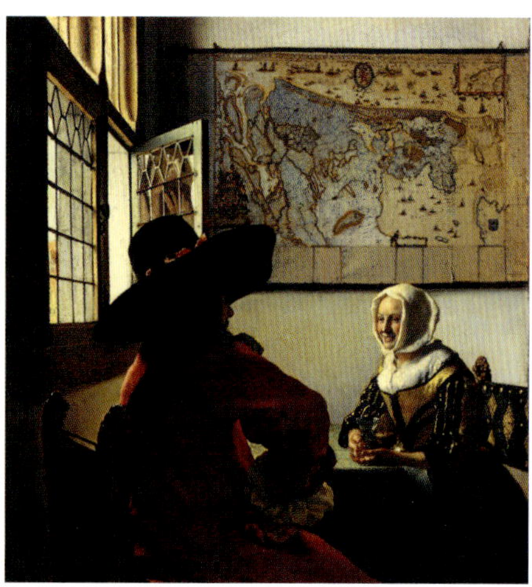

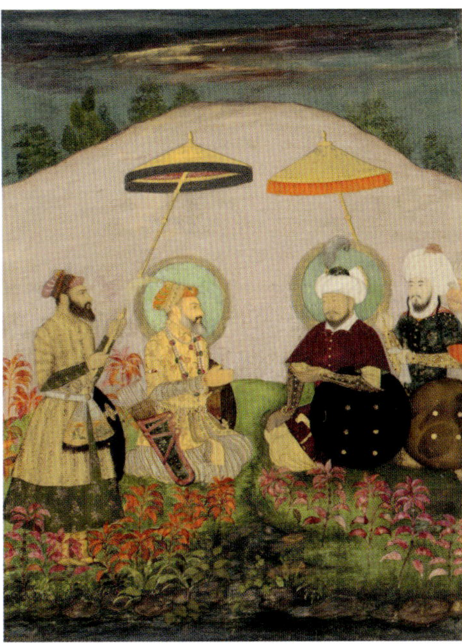

Fig. 25. Mughal, *The Mughal Emperor Shah Jahan with His Ancestor Timur*, ca. 1650–99. Gouache with gold on paper, 6 ½ × 10 ¼ in. (16.6 × 26 cm). Private collection

comes into contact with objects that can bring the past to life. The group inside the vitrine in *Museum Boys* is of a type often depicted by the artist and described as a "fag puddle." The two boys in the painting encounter a scene of exhaustion, a commentary on the role of lust and consumerism in today's world. They have emerged from a similar situation or, after meeting while cruising in a museum, will become the artifacts themselves.

The paintings of Johannes Vermeer at the Frick—*Officer and Laughing Girl* (fig. 24) and *Mistress and Maid* especially—provided the inspiration behind the creation of this painting. The objects drifting in from the two Vermeers into *Museum Boys* (the felt hat, the ruff, the pearl earring), however, are not the only points of connection between the two painters and their work. Famously dubbed "the sphinx of Delft" by the nineteenth-century art critic Théophile Thoré-Bürger, the Dutch master is known for his mysterious compositions. It is unclear how the artist's contemporaries understood them four centuries ago, and his paintings remain riddles for us today. When looking at *Officer and Laughing Girl*, are we witnessing a love story, an erotic encounter, or a financial transaction? Are the paintings truthful descriptions of contemporary habits, or are they imbued with moralistic or deeper meanings? The same questions apply to Toor's *Museum Boys* and to his oeuvre more broadly. Toor—like Vermeer—is not interested, however, in our solving a riddle. He encourages us to explore the domestic worlds he creates for us, setting up a play in front of the viewer. We are inquisitive, delighted, uneasy, aghast, titillated, uncomfortable. As Shakespeare concluded his sonnet: "These offices, so oft as thou wilt look, / Shall profit thee and much enrich thy book." XS

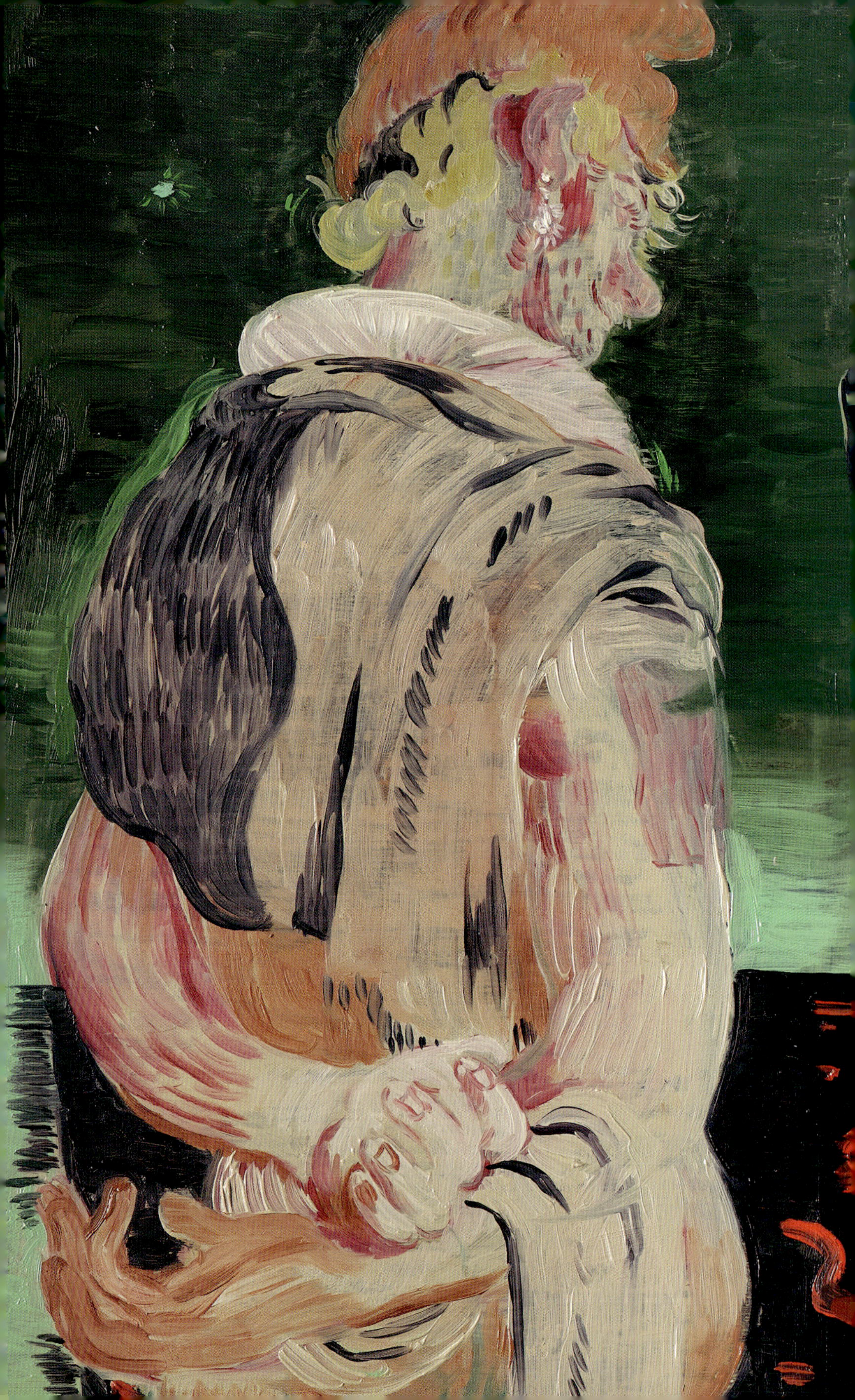

Salman Toor

in Conversation with Christopher Y. Lew

CHRISTOPHER Y. LEW — I was thinking back to the conversations you and I had about twentieth- and twenty-first-century art when we were working on the Whitney show with our co-curator Ambika Trasi. What a contrast to your exhibition at the Frick, where the historical context is vastly different by hundreds of years. What was this experience at the Frick like in terms of that context?

SALMAN TOOR — It was a dream come true but also very intimidating. I got a call from Xavier Salomon, who said they wanted to update the perspective of the Frick historically and asked if I would like to participate and show next to Vermeer. And I said that I would like that very much. The idea was that my work might go well with Vermeer because a lot of it is domestic and dainty and sometimes fairly small. I was a bit self-conscious about showing in a purely European space, but at the same time I was pleased that the Frick had a chance, during its run at the Madison Avenue building, to update its view of canonical painters for a new generation. To choose Queer views of painters like Rembrandt, Vermeer, and Holbein—that was pretty cool.

CYL — So how did you arrive at the *Museum Boys* painting?

ST — My first instinct was to sort of update Vermeer. Vermeer was painting middle-class people in a pretty moralistic social system, and I thought I'd like to paint two boys doing dishes in a very recognizable downtown or Bushwick apartment. But the sketch I first made for it was too literal—just not good enough for Vermeer. So I decided to go the allegorical route and think about the growing super-messy Dutch global trade at the time, the Dutch in Southeast Asia and East Asia.

CYL — And museums are a kind of legacy of that colonial history.

ST — Completely. I wanted to create a fantastical space that has imaginary sculptures and objects in it that recreated the museum context of a linear history, especially because I grew up in Pakistan, where there aren't many museums and there isn't that neat linear history. I wanted to reimagine that and play with it, disturb it, and also think about romance and composition in Vermeer's paintings, where people are deep in conversation or engaged in a kind of mysterious exchange. I wanted that exchange between two characters who

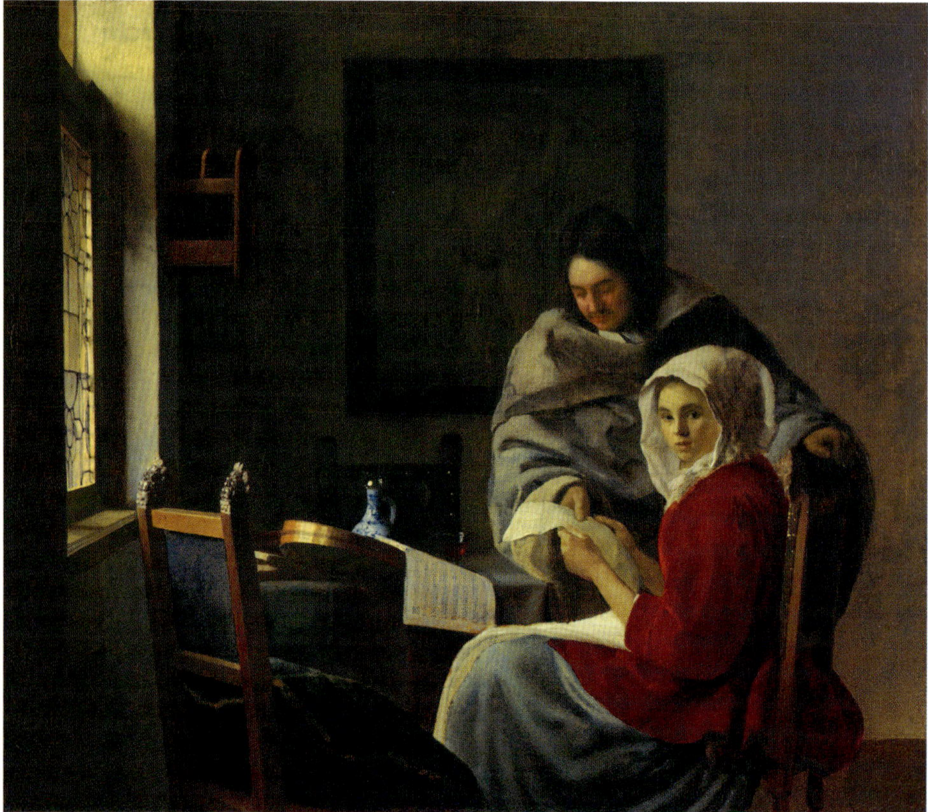

Fig. 26. Johannes Vermeer, *Girl Interrupted at Her Music*, ca. 1658–59. Oil on canvas, 15 ½ × 17 ½ in. (39.4 × 44.5 cm). The Frick Collection, New York

are lost in a labyrinth of objects that ranges from severed-looking heads—I was thinking of various Indigenous cultures—to imagined marble forms resembling more traditional European heroic figures. I wanted the mysterious exchange between the two figures to occur over an object or across a vitrine or a table, as in *Officer and Laughing Girl*. I wanted to ask the question of whether art is a conduit to conversation and understanding or just smoke and mirrors.

CYL – In the Vermeer painting, there is a lot of ambiguity in terms of the figures and their relationships with each other. What's being said? Why is the officer laughing?

ST – I think the insinuation is that it's naughty. There is this sense of anticipation and arrival in both of the Vermeer paintings (figs. 24, 26). Even when the lover is absent, he's there in some way; the letter is arriving, and there is some dramatic turn of events in this romance.

CYL – Similarly, with *Museum Boys*, it feels like it's as much about what's not said.

ST – Absolutely, and I guess that's the Queer part of Vermeer that I like. He is operating in a moralistic society in which the pictures function as a moral release for their owners, who I imagine might have looked at these pictures as slightly off-center romantic comedies, like a movie. But also they're Queering because in societies like that people probably had to work with the kind of nonverbal cues and body language that Queer people have had to use for a long time in the United States and especially in places like Pakistan and South Asia, where those languages are developed to such a great extent and understood so readily by other Queer people because of the dangers of being out. So that was one way of relating to Vermeer.

CYL – *Museum Boys* is also part of what seems to be this ongoing series around museological spaces. Another one I remember is your *Art Room* painting (fig. 27). Can you talk about that and also about what it means for you as a South Asian artist making work at the Frick, to think about both of these things together.

ST – I come from a country that doesn't have as neatly compiled a history as many of these museums that have hoards of treasures from all over the world and have created linear ways of looking at history. It's a privilege to show in a museum that is very linear and to disrupt that a little bit, to reevaluate everyone's position in regards to whose story is most important and urgent and how it should be told. I really enjoyed doing that in this painting. To tell the story of arriving as an immigrant in this country—which is rapidly changing in a post-#MeToo, post-BLM atmosphere—in a dignified way is a huge privilege.

CYL – To move to a lighter topic, I love how fashion functions in your paintings because it breaks them out of time. One starts to ask what period or decade the painting is set in. It's very hard to place.

ST – In the Immigration Paintings (fig. 28) I made for the Whitney show, the people in the paintings are kind of self-presenting. They're conscious of presenting themselves to be legible to a Western sensibility. How much English or other Western language is spoken here? What is the hygiene of this person?

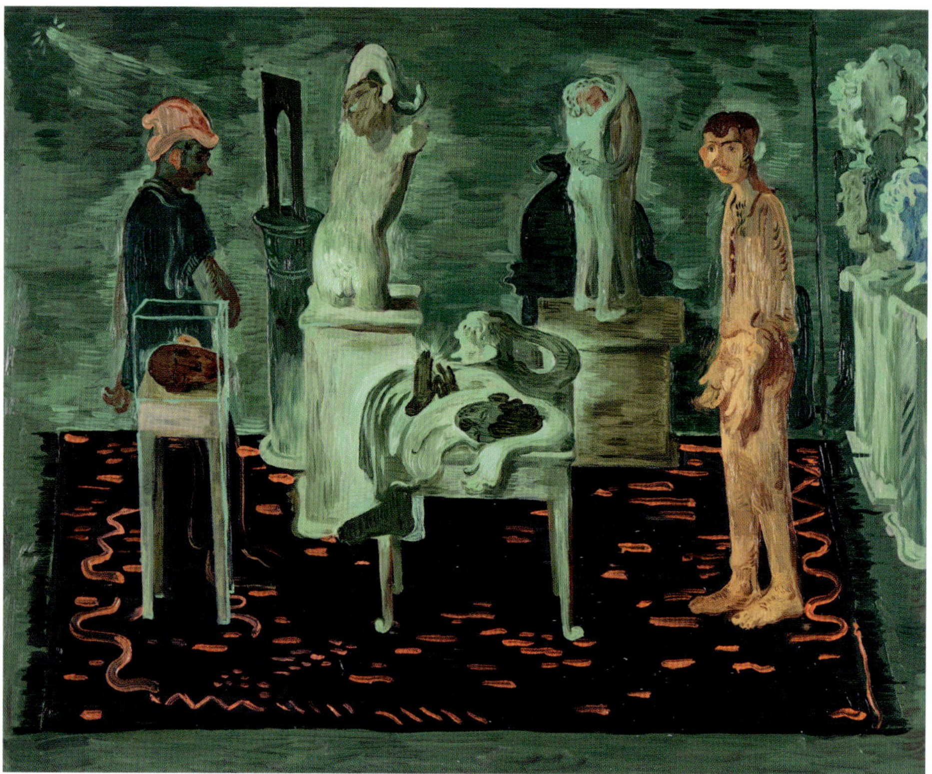

Fig. 27. Salman Toor, *Art Room*, 2020. Oil on panel, 20 × 24 in. (50.8 × 61 cm). Marieluise Hessel Collection, Hessel Museum of Art, Center for Curatorial Studies, Bard College, Annandale-on-Hudson, New York

How friendly could that person be? Would it be easier for them to assimilate or not? I enjoy working with these questions.

CYL — I'm glad you brought up the Immigration Paintings because in some ways there are similarities between them and *Museum Boys*. There's the expression, at least of the figure on the right-hand side of the painting, that's not very happy. It's more of a dour, downcast face. It also reminds me of the figures from the Immigration Paintings because of the emphasis on objects, whether they are, say, the possessions of someone crossing a border or what we might call the surreal objects in *Museum Boys*. There is this relationship between figures and objects in both.

ST — For sure. I like paintings in which people are quietly doing something, not engaging with the viewer. They invite the viewer to be something of a voyeur. I think of the expression on the main figure, the brown body and this kind of brown boy/man, as apocalyptic chic, like he's someone who has gone through something to get here. I had this idea that he's encountering some spirit of a colonial clown who is inviting him to figure out the riddle of this object, which is something that I call a "fag puddle." I've done a bunch of these. The first was in our show, although I think I called it *Parts and Things*. I think of these fag puddles as heaps of exhaustion and lust. And they're usually kind of leaky. It's just a bunch of things that I'm thinking about that I turn into this kind of pathetic and funny heap. It can sometimes have a flag on top of it like it's this ruined country or something that just has no more energy.

CYL — Yeah, it's often body parts and objects. But this one is different. It's a full body, like a person in a vitrine.

ST — Yeah, a person stuffed very uncomfortably into a vitrine but not struggling, just lying there. Sometimes, I'll have bedsheets or laundry and hands and feet. To me, these are parts that can be combined to form a different whole each time. The urinal was included on a whim. I'd been thinking about the Duchamp urinal and wanted to put it somewhere in my paintings. I wanted some sense of insolence in the very clean, august space of the Frick's Vermeer gallery. Talking about bodily fluids and dirty things in the popular imagination, like cruisy spaces and places that the characters in Vermeer's paintings would find really vulgar, fulfilled that need for me. And of course it provides a fag puddle with leakages, which is essential.

I wanted to place the urinal the way that Duchamp had placed it—upside down—because I always imagined it as the silhouette of the Madonna. It does look very much like that. And next to it is an article I've been putting in many of my fag puddles—kind of an eighteenth-century shoe or a Cinderella type of thing/shoe with a cutesy bow. I think it goes well with the urinal because it's so dainty and very femme.

CYL — I love that contrast, but can we go back to our apocalyptic boy/man? He seems to be missing pants and a shoe. It appears as though he's been through a lot.

ST — He was supposed to have pants, but then I decided he shouldn't. Later, I thought maybe his legs should be covered, maybe he'll have really high stockings. But that wasn't working aesthetically because the carpet underneath

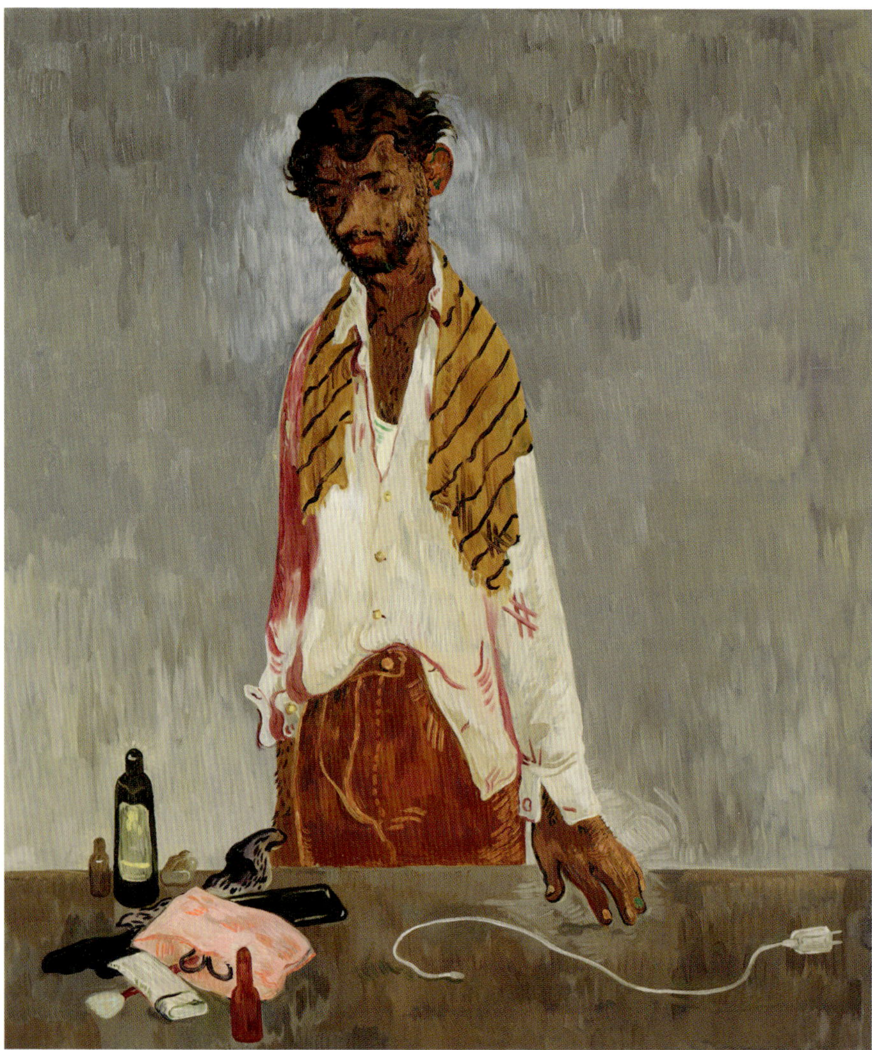

Fig. 28. Salman Toor, *Man with Face Creams and Phone Plug,* 2019. Oil on canvas, 43 × 35 ¾ in. (109.2 × 90.8 cm). Whitney Museum of American Art, New York; purchase, with funds from the Painting and Sculpture Committee

was so dark, and his leg looked like it was missing. These were some of the decisions that led me to take his pants off. And I wanted the assertion of his penis in this and to create a sense of humor with his kind of clown nose and a single shoe.

CYL — And what about the other figure, who seems to be much more of an observer of the scene, almost like a proxy for the viewer.

ST – I wanted him to be forbidding with his dark smile. Originally, I wanted him to be the size of the other figure. But then I responded to the Vermeer, where the officer is much larger—we can't see his face, only the back of his shoulder. But I wanted that other figure to be the smiley one in the composition and look like he is wearing some kind of shawl and tattered scarves and what I thought of as a ruff, along with an earring. I wanted him to be kind of welcoming this other person and giving him a dark, riddle-ish smile.

CYL – Yeah, there is a powerful ambiguity to the picture.

ST – Part of the intimidation of showing next to Vermeer was that my painting was never full enough. I felt I could always add more stuff. So I created the busts and sculpture in the back, letting my hand be playful and just do whatever. I ended up creating a kind of Islamic gravestone on top of a sort of marble plinth. At the time, it looked to me like a seventeenth-century European curly-haired marble bust, a globe or a mirror. And then there's the bust behind the Islamic tombstone, a Buddhist bust, in profile. These are action-like, mythological-looking sculptures that are all mixed up. They don't even look like bodies anymore. And then, gratuitously, I added what looks like a dildo on top of a marble plinth.

CYL – The fag puddle was not enough! One final question: What have you learned from making this painting and exhibiting it alongside Vermeer? Were there any direct takeaways?

ST – Yeah, nothing was enough. If I were to redo this painting, I'd take out some of the stuff. I love the painting as it is, but it was definitely a consequence of nothing ever being enough for Vermeer. But it was such a privilege to show in that gallery next to those two paintings. I learned that showing alongside European Old Masters, Queering that history, can piss some people off. Which is what makes it worthwhile.

4

Toyin Ojih Odutola

The Listener

2021
Charcoal, pastel, and chalk on linen over Dibond panel, 84 × 50 in. (213.4 × 127 cm)
Courtesy the artist and Jack Shainman Gallery, New York

The Listener belongs to a series of monumental drawings that chronicle an imagined ancient African civilization ruled by the Eshu, a class of Queer women warriors. In this fictive Black society, heterosexuality is forbidden, homosexuality is compulsory, and the women are served by the Koba, humanoid male laborers the Eshu created. Ojih Odutola's works in this series are presented as printed scans of fragile rock tablets bearing images of this civilization, unearthed in the present day in an archaeological dig in central Nigeria, with the artist posing as the director overseeing excavations. Some forty drawings of this group were presented in *A Countervailing Theory*,[1] an exhibition in which the suite of works recounted the tale of an Eshu warrior, Akanke, and Aldo, a Koba laborer, who break their society's rules by coupling and bearing offspring. The transgression eventually brings the Eshu's system to an end.

Whether and where exactly *The Listener* fits into the larger narrative of the series is not obvious. Larger than life-size, the seated Eshu warrior (pronouns: they/them) in *The Listener* peers out with sparkling eyes, white irises on black corneas. Like all of the drawings in the series, the composition is created through the layering of dry media—pastel, chalk, and charcoal—to make white and gray marks on a black ground. Subtle variations in color, texture, and the handling of materials distinguish the forms of the body from the landscape. The staff—a weapon—rests at the crook of the elbow, and their hands are free. Dark, fitted clothing covering the torso to the tops of the legs and from the knees downward leaves exposed the figure's arms, shoulders, and thighs. The skin is mottled in gray and white, like sunlight seen through leafy trees or reflections in a running brook. The drawing's most intricate handling of materials can be seen in the metallic jewelry worn at the ear and nose. With its evident facture and physical traces of the artist's hand marshalling varied media, the overall effect of the drawing contradicts the pretense of a printed scan. The discrepancy points to the capacity of artists to make myths, to tell viewers what to see and believe.

"[To listen] is an act of love,"[2] Ojih Odutola has said, and it is also one of power: "Choosing to be quiet is its own defiant power, and to let others speak isn't a small courtesy, it's an act of sovereignty." In the artist's text accompanying *A Countervailing Theory*, the act of listening becomes an "unthinkable" deed when it bridges two unequal classes:

> At some point, after all he has learned and accumulated in their travels, Aldo begins to understand the system's unfairness, feeling compelled to

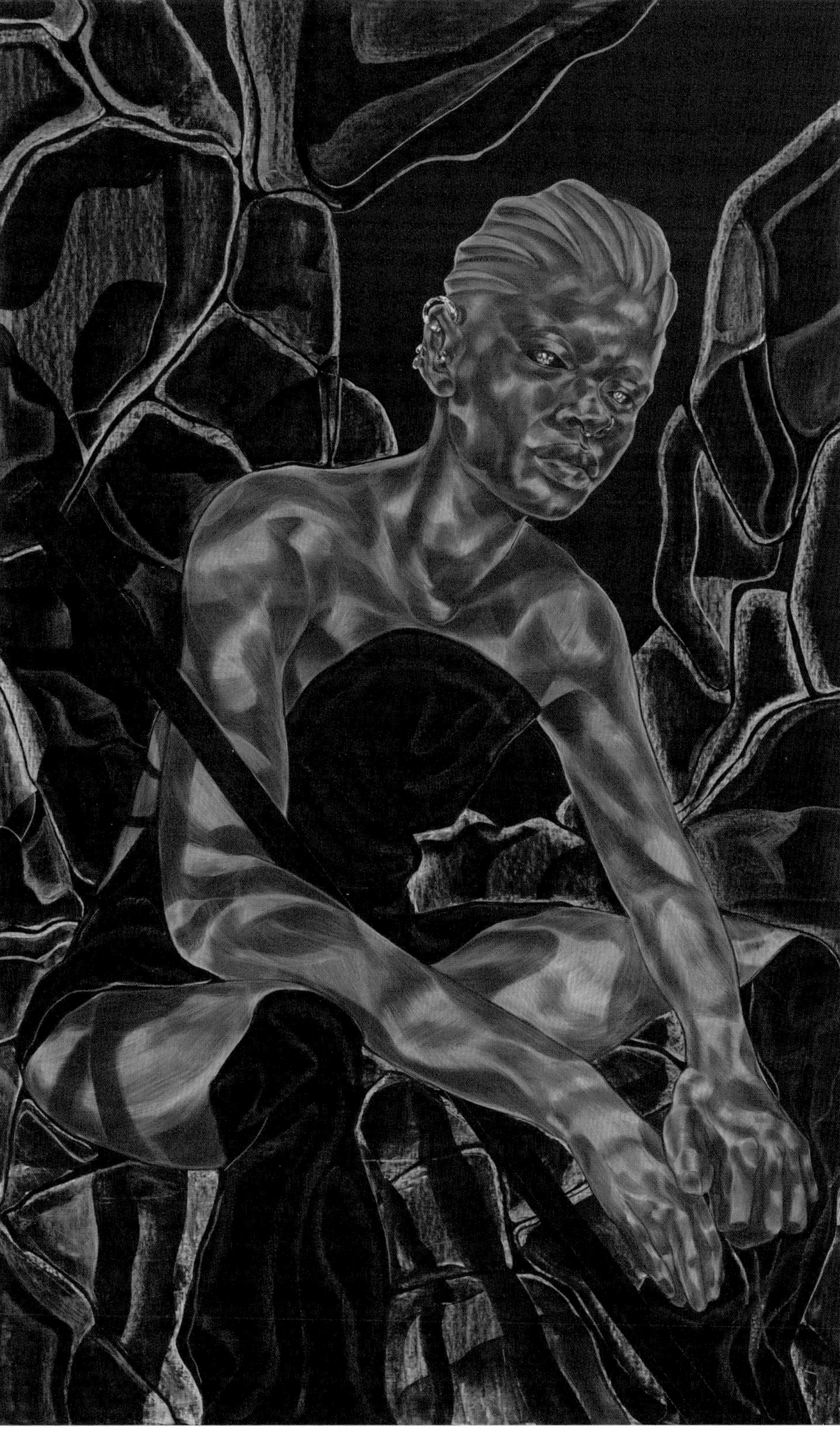

> tell Akanke his story and how they might go about enacting change. She does the unthinkable: she listens, comes to terms with her own position within the system and eventually agrees.[3]

With eyes directed outward, the figure in *The Listener* addresses the viewer, their act of listening both a gift of love and an exertion of power.

Encountering *The Listener* in the Rembrandt room at Frick Madison may at first seem jarring to some visitors, as the contemporary work does not correspond in obvious ways to Rembrandt's *Self-Portrait* (fig. 29), the largest and arguably most famous of the artist's dozens of self-portraits, or his *Nicolaes Ruts* (fig. 31). Reproductions of *The Listener* in publications like this volume cannot convey its full visual force: the seven-foot drawing nearly dwarfs Rembrandt's pictures. Ojih Odutola's and Rembrandt's works operate within distinct aesthetic vocabularies—in scale, palette, materials, approaches to rendering bodies in space—a disjuncture that signals artistic autonomy, the embrace of difference, and resistance to conformity. In the range of Ojih Odutola's artistic production, polychrome portraits like *Pregnant* (fig. 32)—in their aristocratic grandeur, narrative drama, and engagement with conventions of beauty and traditions of Western art—appear more commensurate with Rembrandt and his legacies. Not so with *The Listener*, which claims independence and conjures a world in which Rembrandt never existed or has not yet existed, a world that is indifferent to his existence. Yet they listen, sovereign in their individuality.

The works share some elements. The trappings of authority and power in Rembrandt's *Self-Portrait*—the figure's monumental scale, seated as if enthroned, the semblance of a cape and scepter—are an illusion, an invention of the artist like Ojih Odutola's fictive world. Rembrandt was bankrupt by the time he painted it. His *Nicolaes Ruts* celebrates the fur-clad fur trader, who has an air of self-satisfaction as he extends a slip of paper, as if another bill of sale of his profitable business. His pride was fleeting; soon after the portrait was made, Ruts too declared bankruptcy. Especially in recent years, the works of Rembrandt and other seventeenth-century Dutch artists have been recontextualized within the exploitative systems of power in this period of world history, above all the enslavement of Africans and Indigenous people in the service of global trade that built the affluence of Rembrandt and his Amsterdam patrons. *The Listener* and their civilization may seem to present a fantasy of retribution, a just inversion of the world represented by Rembrandt's

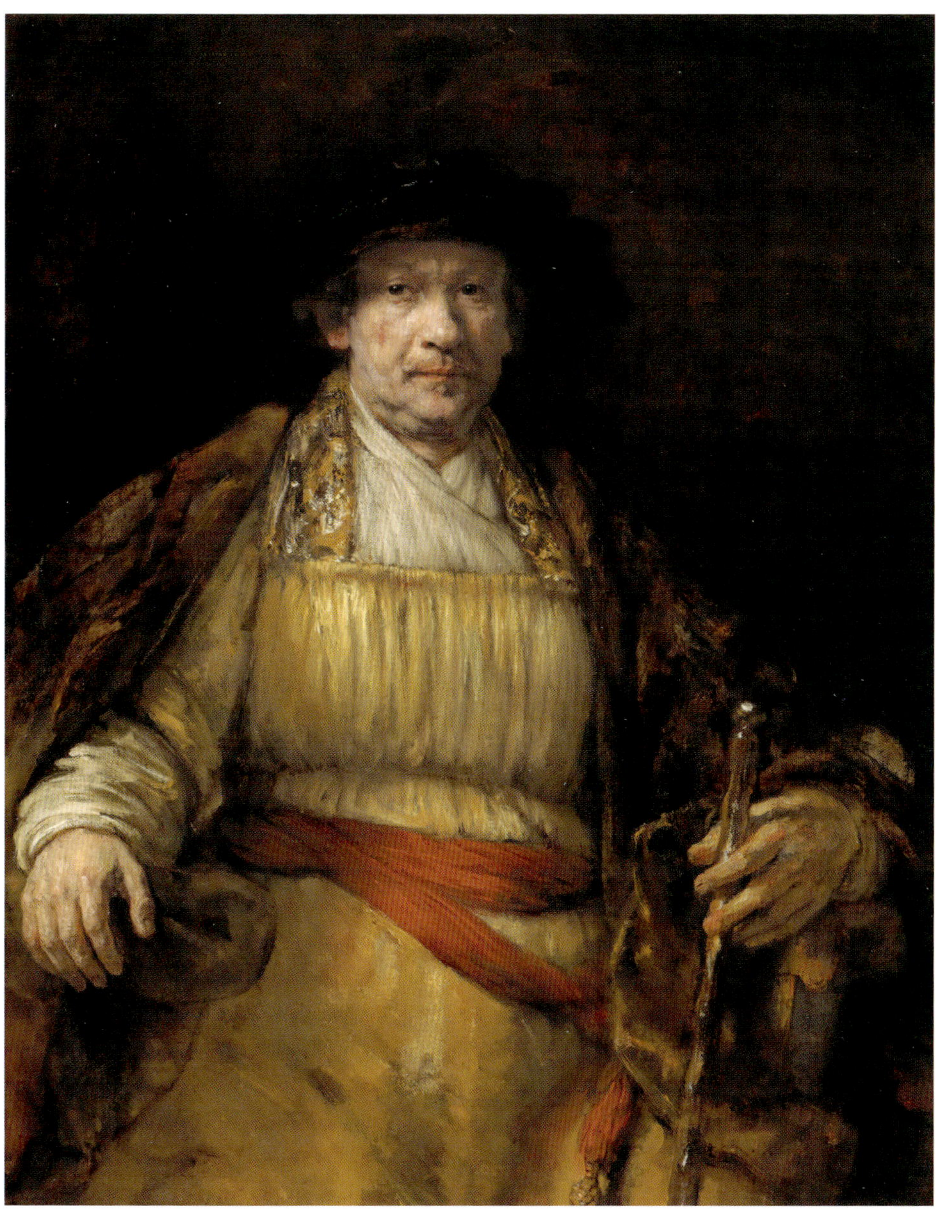

Fig. 29. Rembrandt Harmensz. van Rijn, *Self-Portrait*, 1658. Oil on canvas, 52 ⅝ × 40 ⅞ in. (133.7 × 103.8 cm). The Frick Collection, New York

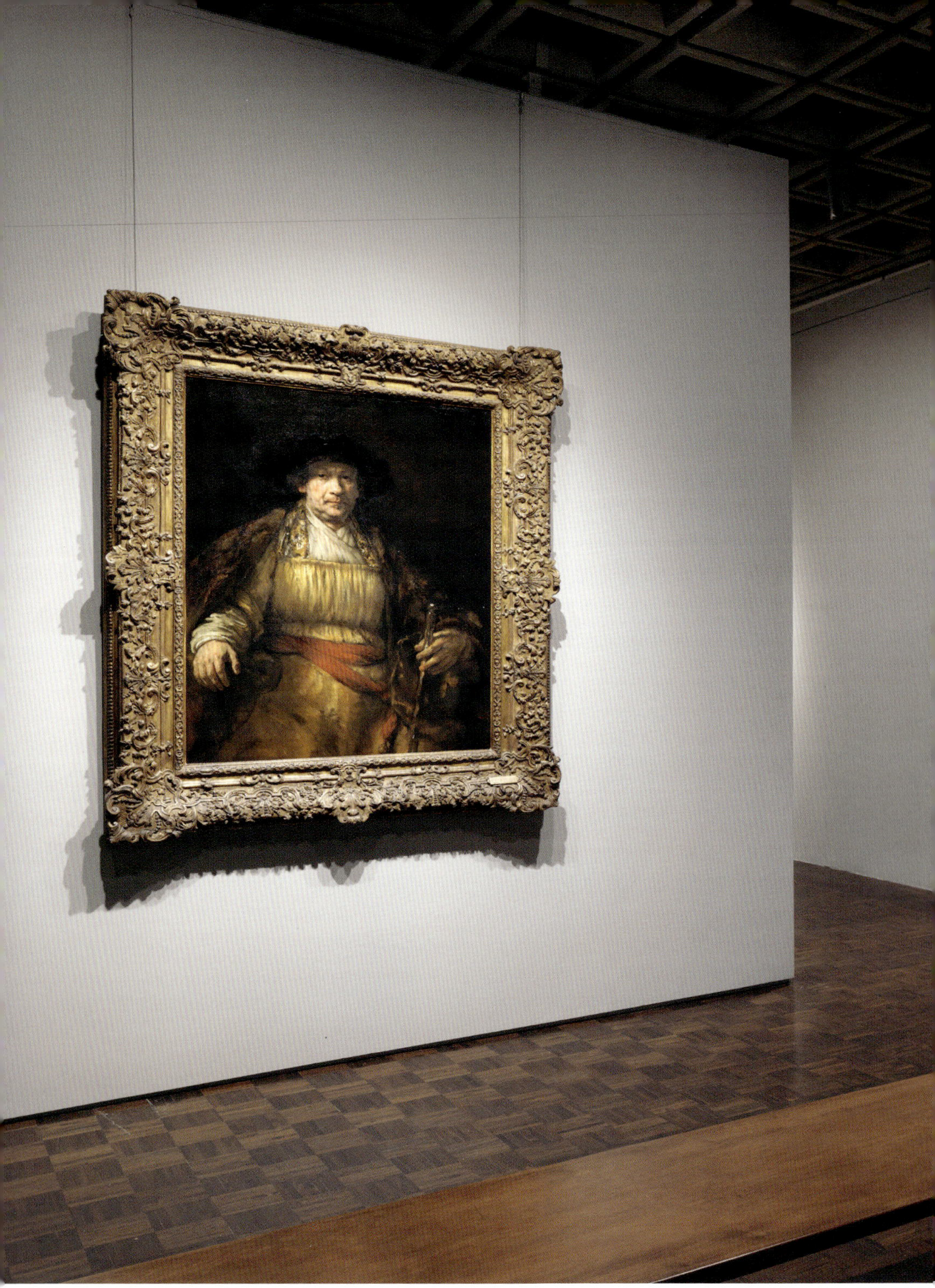

Fig. 30. Installation view of *Living Histories*
Left: Rembrandt Harmensz. van Rijn, *Self-Portrait*, 1658 (fig. 29)
Right: Toyin Ojih Odutola, *The Listener*, 2021 (cat. 4)

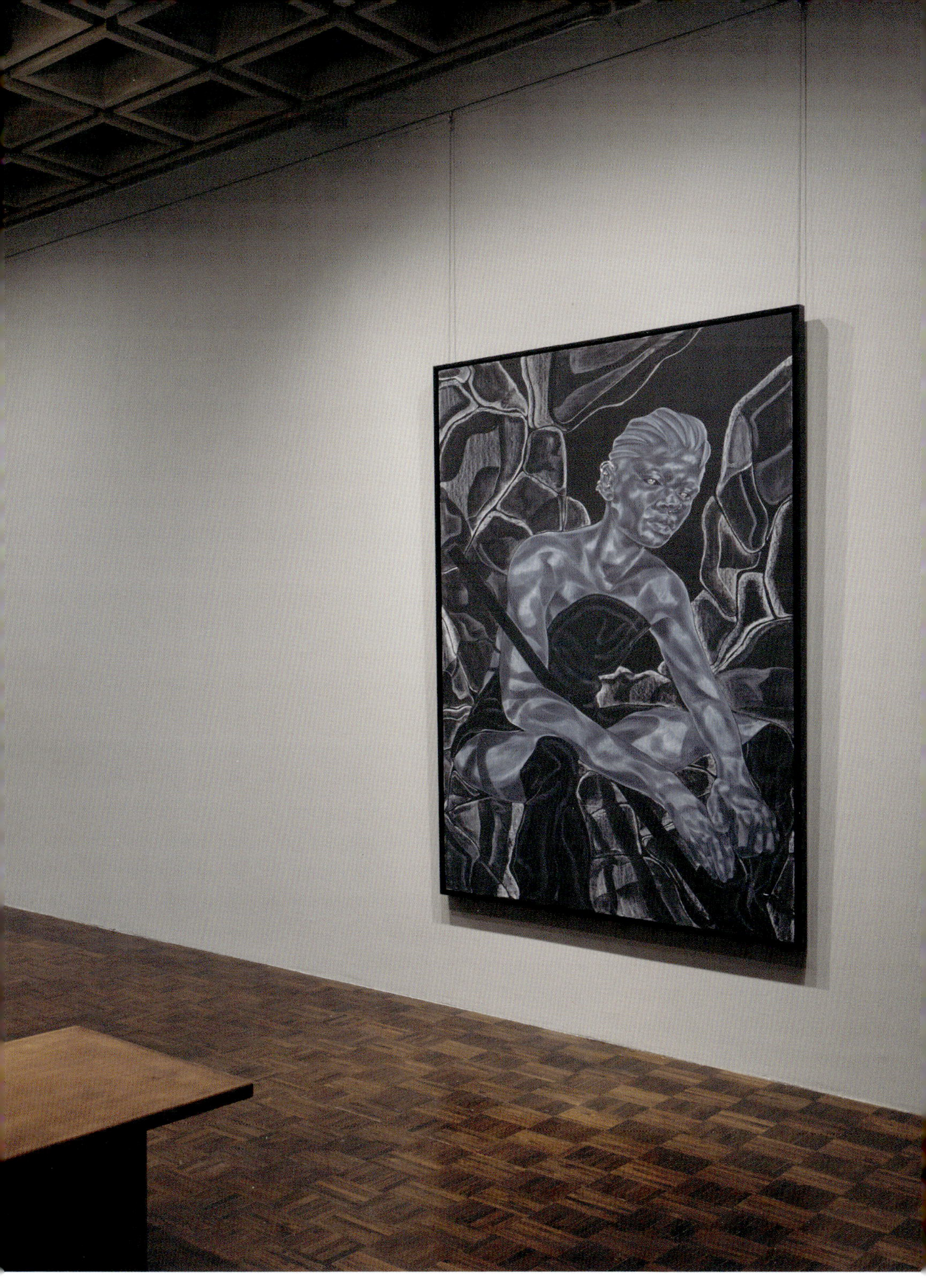

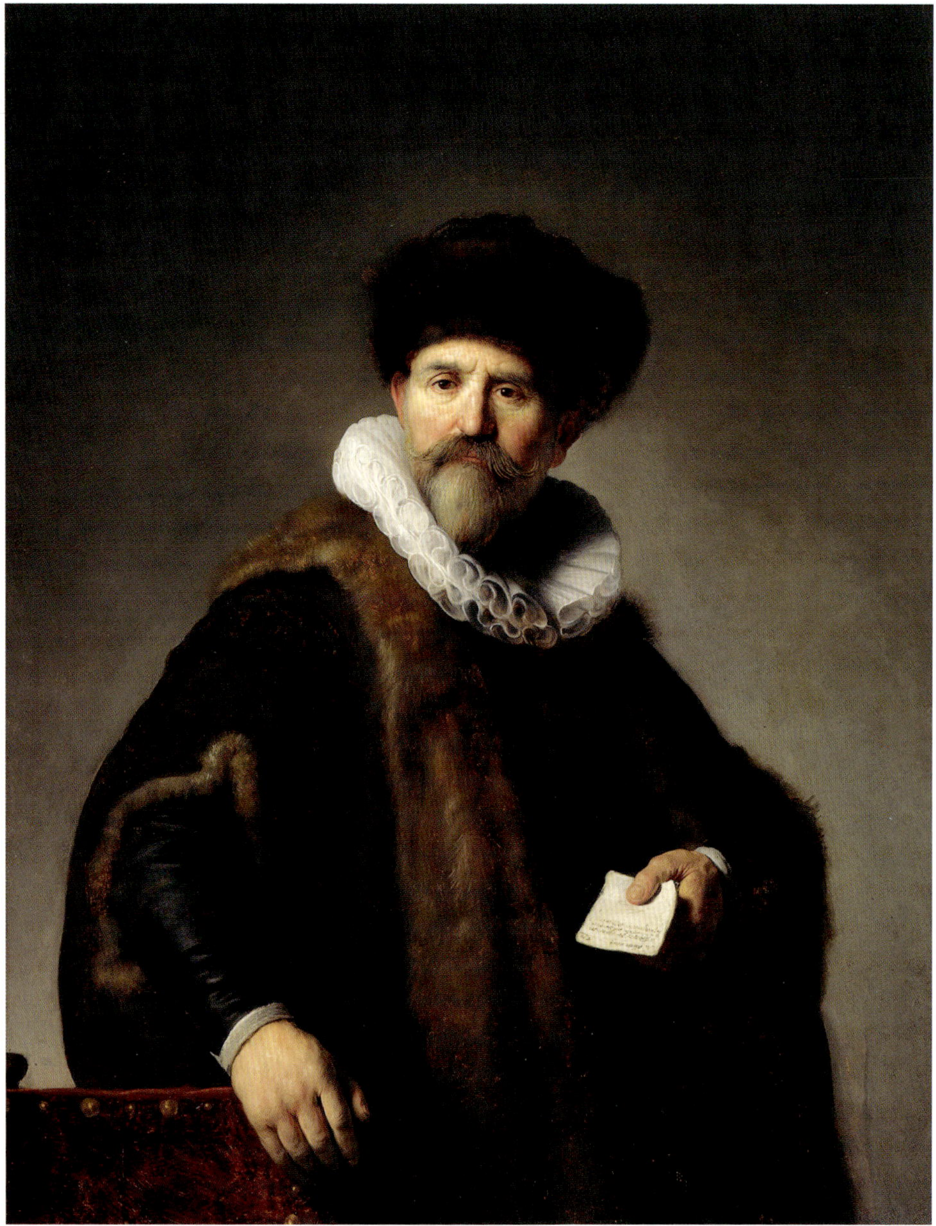

Fig. 31. Rembrandt Harmensz. van Rijn, *Nicolaes Ruts*, 1631. Oil on panel, 46 × 34 ⅜ in. (116.8 × 87.3 cm). The Frick Collection, New York

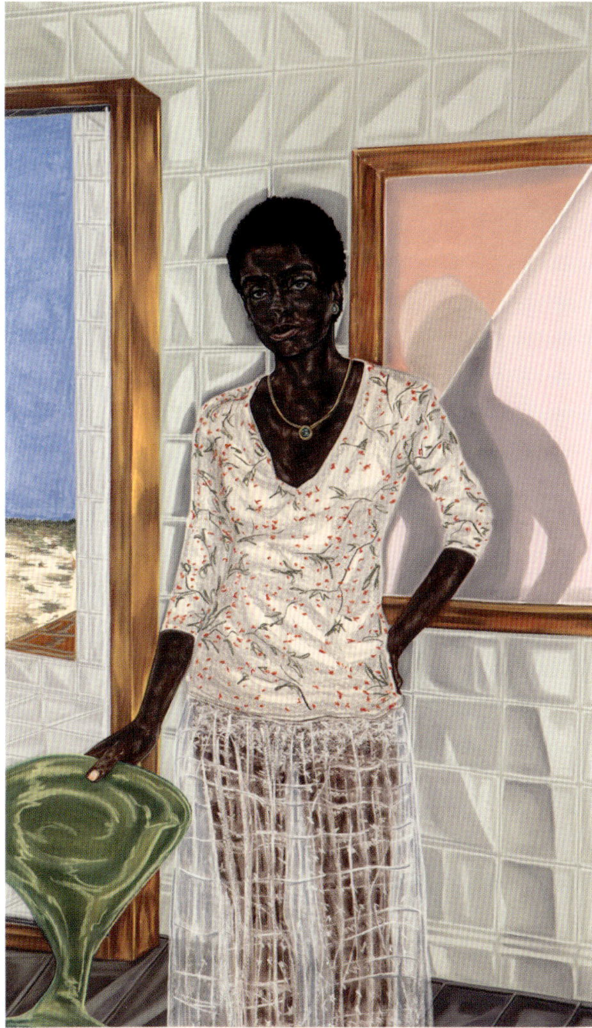

Fig. 32. Toyin Ojih Odutola, *Pregnant*, 2017. Charcoal, pastel, and graphite on paper, 74 ½ × 42 in. (189.2 × 106.7 cm). Hood Museum of Art, Dartmouth; purchased through the Florence and Lansing Porter Moore 1937 Fund

art, putting Queer Black women in positions of power in place of historical European men. But as Ojih Odutola cautions—in the conclusion of *The Tale of Akanke and Aldo* (and see her interview with Jason Reynolds in this publication)—representation itself, swapping the demographics of those in power, is no solution. The problem is the system itself, the exploitation of one class of people by another, no matter who they are. From their mythic perch, like an otherworldly visitor who prompts profound reflection on the world we live in, *The Listener* speaks volumes. **AN**

Notes

1. Toyin Ojih Odutola et al., *Toyin Ojih Odutola: A Countervailing Theory*, exh. cat. (The Curve, Barbican Art Gallery, London; Kunsten Museum of Modern Art, Aalborg; and Hirshhorn Museum and Sculpture Garden, Washington, DC), 2020–21.
2. Ibid., 47.
3. Ibid., 12–13.

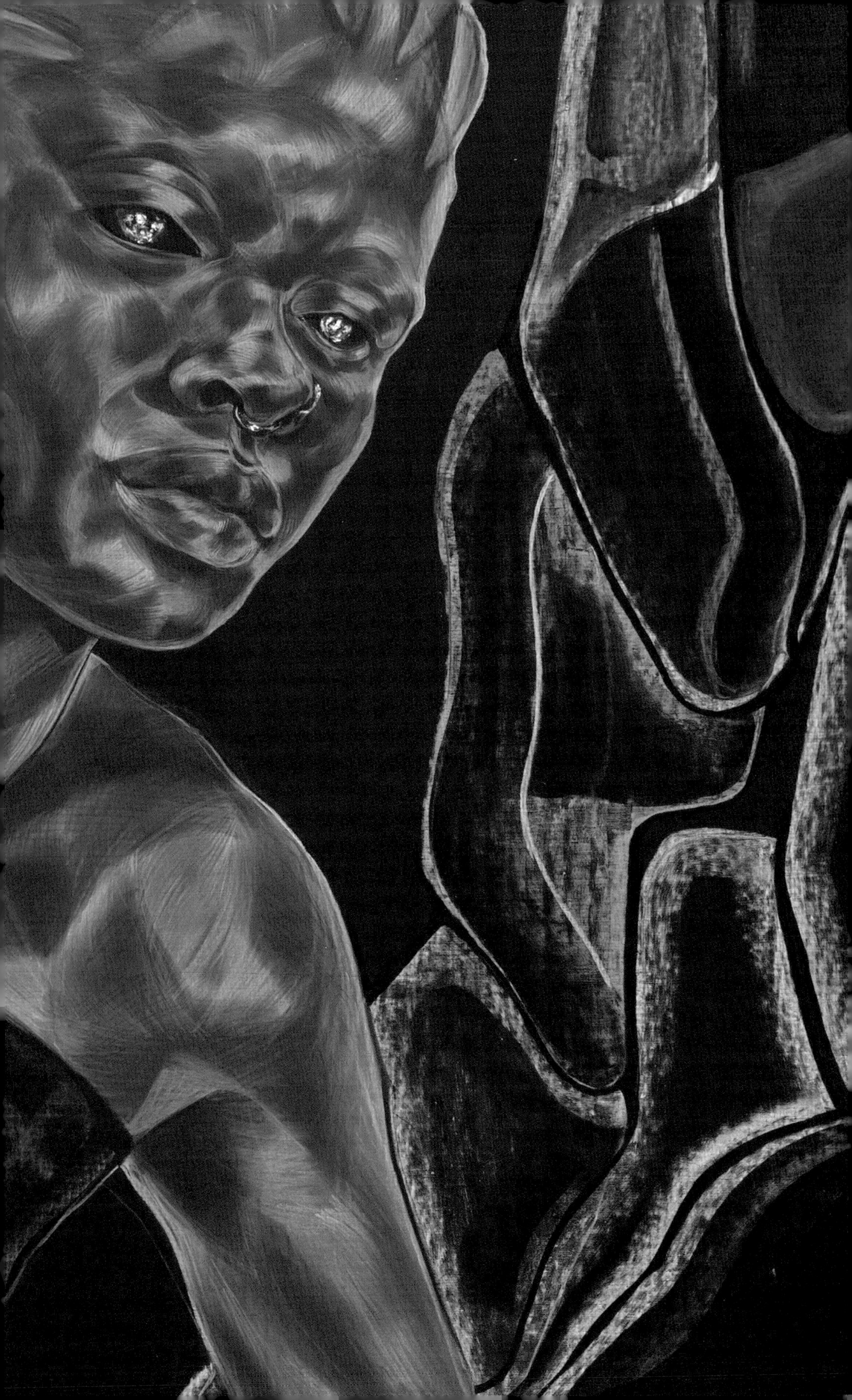

Toyin Ojih Odutola
in Conversation with Jason Reynolds

JASON REYNOLDS — When I was asked to do this interview, my initial thought was about the title *Living Histories: Queer Views and Old Masters*—the term *Old Masters* does wild things to me!

TOYIN OJIH ODUTOLA — Yeah, I know exactly what you mean. It's still something I'm processing. I cannot say *Old Masters* un-ironically. I find the idea of mastery really misplaced. You've mastered this skill; thus, we give you the appropriate respect you deserve. I think that's a very misguided and misapplied view of what art can be. I don't see myself as a master, and I don't want to be. I'm a perpetual student. I think the reason I wanted to do this project was to show that this isn't mastery but an emphasis on conversation. I hope this project shows the variety that is lacking in "old mastery" thought and teaching. The "old mastery" I was contending with was the legacy of Rembrandt.

JR – *Old Master* is such a loaded term. In my world as a writer, we use the word *classics*. So, my question to you is: Who are your classics?

TOO – Drawings by Barkley L. Hendricks. Prints by Kitagawa Utamaro. Sculpture by Elizabeth Catlett. Architecture by Demas Nwoko. Varied places for learning. When it comes to "classics," I think about this idea in conversation with contemporary works. How reverence is the past in dialogue with the present. A reshaping ritual not to maintain but to measure and progress. For me, it's changing the landscape of culture in our own way. "Living histories"—we're writing them as we live, by the choices we're making through intersections and encounters. Still, appetites for revision are welcome.

You see it in the language of institutions right now doing similar programming where they want to fill in the gaps. There's a part of me that's excited about this time because it's redefining the language and what is deemed important in these institutions. But it's a thin line as the market for revision is more the driver than listening to the language of figuration as it is reformulating itself. Part of what I knew going into this Frick project was that I would have to work through that oppressive language and try to make it something more freeing. I'm always thinking about creating more options. I couldn't just regurgitate the same ideas about mastery.

To listen is very hard. It's a skill we're always learning. There's a lot of cacophony, and I fear institutions like this chatter and can get so distracted

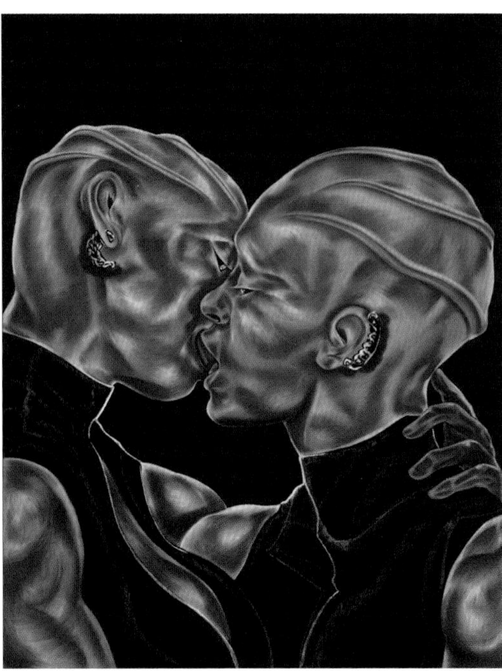

Fig. 33. Toyin Ojih Odutola, *A Parting Gift; Hers and Hers, Only*, 2019. Pastel, charcoal, and chalk on board, 40 × 30 in. (101.6 × 76.2 cm)

by it and occupied with it they're not really listening. There's a distinct dialect we're all speaking, and you have to acclimate yourself. You have to understand where it's coming from and where it wants to go. This activity takes time.

JR – There's a literacy that is needed, a basic literacy that many of us don't have anymore, maybe never had. The writer Kiese Laymon has this concept about revision as a way of life. And when I was thinking about *A Countervailing Theory* and *The Listener*, especially when up against—I hate to say "up against"—but next to or in space with Rembrandt, I think about this idea around revision. And by revision, I don't mean a correction but "seeing again," reimagining. You reimagine in this particular context a civilization of women warriors with male laborers who work for them.

TOO – The world of *A Countervailing Theory* is a means to highlight how corrupt a system is by flipping the script. People can get distracted by the flipping of the script and misunderstand that the plot is still driven by the same systemic injustices. I'm highlighting the fact that the system is the same, and you're distracted by representation, which is where we are now with the overemphasis on identity. I feel there's a lot of disillusionment around the Black figure and the forms we can take in art, how it is used, co-opted in all avenues. I don't want to confuse our sense of ourselves with how we relate to our world and what we want for the world. These are separate things.

I believe art is a reminder. If anything, our power's in reminding. In this room, there are narratives around the monumentality of power and who gets

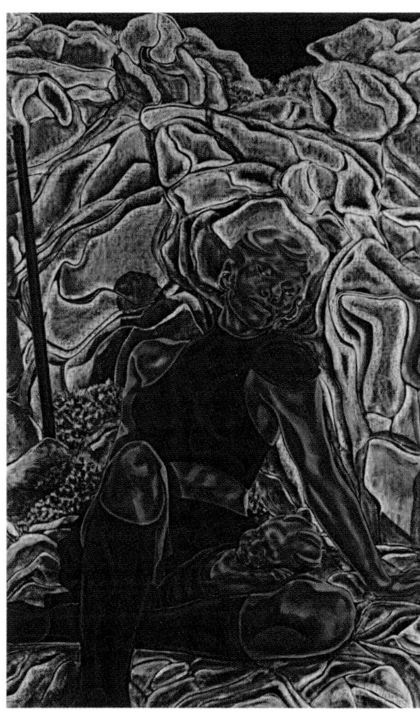

Fig. 34. Toyin Ojih Odutola, *New Found Land; A Vow*, 2020. Charcoal, pastel, and chalk on linen over Dibond panel, 84 × 50 in. (218.4 × 132 cm)

to control and command things. Those who see the Rembrandt portraits will witness an argument for lonesome power, and those who see *The Listener* are engaging with a figure who embodies collective power and chooses to apply that power differently.

JR – As a viewer of the two works, they feel the same, but don't. When I look at the Rembrandt, I say, "Man, look at this monumental regal painting." I say the same thing when I look at *The Listener*, but it doesn't feel the same. That could be contextualized around my issues with whiteness; it could be all me, projection. We know Rembrandt's *Self-Portrait* was painted toward the end of his life, when he had nothing. He was not this regal thing.

TOO – We know this story. I don't know how many people know my story. People write our narratives for us, and I find that very uncomfortable. Distracted with identity again. I'm sure there are ideas around Rembrandt that have morphed over time. But this is happening to my story in real time.

When I get into these programs, there's always a moment where I ask myself: "Who does this serve exactly? Is this the right way for me, the right creative voyage I'm choosing to go on?" Because there were many times I questioned it when I was making this work.

JR – I don't always know. And I don't know if you feel this way—I don't ever feel like I sit down at the page without the weight of responsibility. Even though I know that representation is not the be-all and end-all, I've seen moments where it

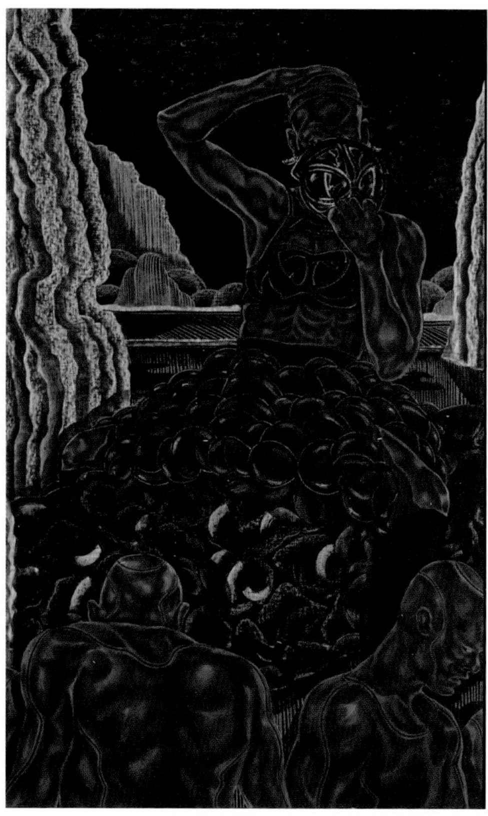

Fig. 35. Toyin Ojih Odutola, *Routine Inspection*, 2019. Charcoal, pastel, and chalk on linen over Dibond panel, 84 × 50 in. (213.4 × 127 cm)

works. I think it's a nuanced discussion, because I'm working with kids. So when I'm writing something that's representative, and if some little Black girl looks at this book and says, like, "Yo, that's me, and I feel differently about myself," then I don't know if that's a loss. Even though it wasn't your intention, if I'm sitting in that room and I'm looking at these images and representationally they make me feel something: for me, when I look at your work, any of your work, it always feels like the light's coming from the inside, like the light is internal.

TOO — I definitely feel like my experience of representation has been hollow. I find much of my time is explaining my situation, my "story." And there's less room for conversation around craft and concepts of picture-making. As a Nigerian coming to this country, I was really excited about the possibility of the project that is America and was thinking about how we as artists have documented this project over time. But then I began to ask myself whether what I wanted was aligned with what an artist is purported to be, or rather an artist's role in a society.

When you think artist, you think Rembrandt, and that's all business. Being in that room, seeing how frail he was in his self-portrait—this is a man who's donning the costume of Renaissance lore to feel good about his situation. You can't not relate to that, but, at the same time, do I want that? Do I want to feel like I'm harkening to that lineage by virtue of the juxtaposition of our work? In the end, Rembrandt is over there, and I'm here—that's the certainty I have, and I'm okay with that. The language of *A Countervailing Theory*, in craft and conception, felt very ancestral when I was making it. I gather my strength from that. It comes from a place within me.

I'm holding space for all the ancestors. As a creative person, I gotta juggle Rembrandt's narrative and also the psychology it demands. No lie, I feel a type of way about that: like why do I need to know this dude?

JR – That was my real first question.

TOO – This doesn't mean I shouldn't consider his choices of mark-making and the potential to learn from that. But what of those who will enter this space? What will they consider and learn from? There may be a diversity of viewership, which inspires me. An opportunity for whoever visits to experience something different that's for them despite this institution. I'm hoping when young people see this work they will be aware of how this is also speculative. He's donning an idea of being a master, saying, "See, I'm one of the guys, I'm one of the chosen ones."

JR – It's all just the imagination. He literally has painted his imagination.

TOO – And this is what's so sad: of all the imaginary capacity he had, he just imagined himself to be a master. *The Listener* is many people in one. They are multifarious, they contain many stories. This is evidenced on the surface of their skin, the many people they embody, and in the landscape around them. They're a master of none among many while Rembrandt is alone on a crumbling pedestal of his making.

JR – That is sad. You imagined a whole new world, a whole civilization; and he was like, I need a tabard and a fancy hat and I'm good.

I know that it's a complex thing, and I honestly don't care how you feel about any of this because the truth is that we need you in the world and we're grateful you're in the world. We're grateful this work is in the world. It does what it does for us.

TOO – Appreciate you, Jason.

Artist Biographies

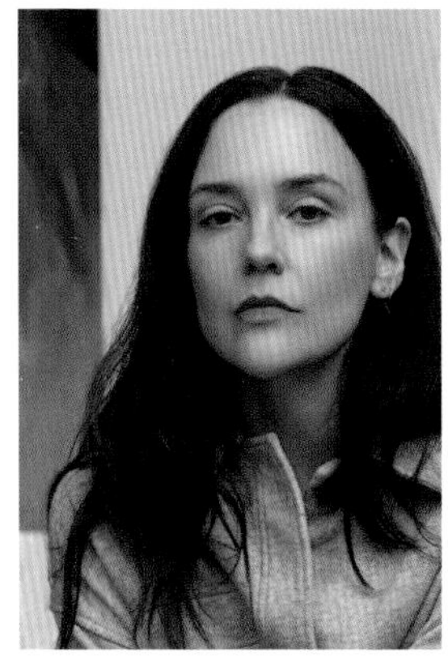

Jenna Gribbon (b. 1978) was born in Knoxville, Tennessee. Her work is in the collections of the Dallas Museum of Art, the New Orleans Museum of Art, the Rubell Museum in Miami, and the Brant Foundation in New York. Gribbon was recently the subject of a solo exhibition at Collezione Maramotti, Reggio Emilia, and her work has been featured in exhibitions at the Modern Art Museum of Fort Worth; the Museum of Modern Art, Warsaw; the Museum of Contemporary Art Jacksonville; the Kurpfälzisches Museum, Heidelberg; and the FLAG Art Foundation, New York. A monograph of her work was published by GNYP Gallery in 2021. She received her MFA from Hunter College. She lives in New York.

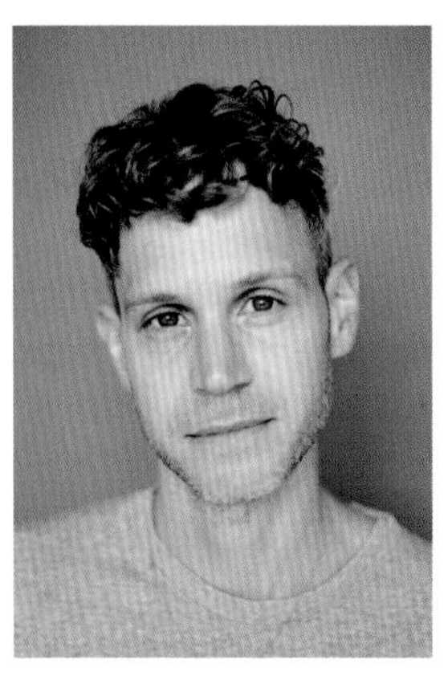

Doron Langberg (b. 1985) was born in Yokneam Moshava, Israel. Recent solo exhibitions include *Give Me Love* at Victoria Miro, London (2021), and *Doron Langberg* at the Rubell Museum, Miami (2022–23). His work was also featured in *A Place for Me: Figurative Painting Now* at the ICA Boston (2022), in *Fire, Figure, Fantasy* at the ICA Miami (2022), in *Any Distance between Us* at the RISD Museum in Providence (2021–22), and in *Intimacy: New Queer Art from Berlin and Beyond* at Berlin's Schwules Museum (2020–21). His work is in the collections of the Baltimore Museum of Art; ICA Miami; ICA Boston; the Pennsylvania Academy of the Fine Arts, Philadelphia; the Rennie Museum, Vancouver; and the Rubell Museum, Miami, among others. Langberg received his MFA from Yale University. He lives in New York.

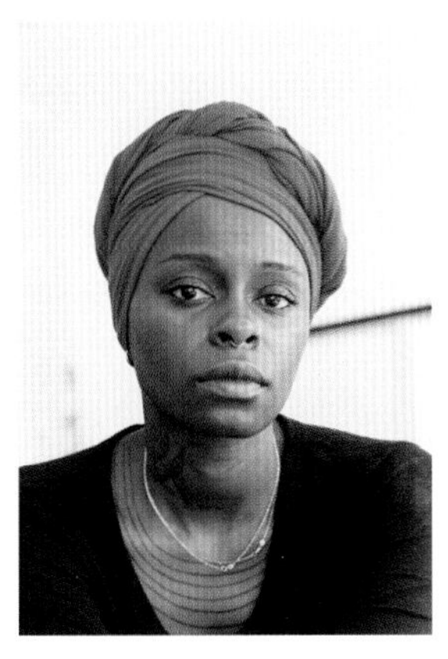

Toyin Ojih Odutola (b. 1985) was born in Ile-Ife, Nigeria, and moved to Alabama as a child. Her first solo museum exhibition in New York, *To Wander Determined*, was held at the Whitney Museum of American Art in 2017–18. In late 2020, London's Barbican Art Gallery presented *A Countervailing Theory*, which later traveled to the Kunsten Museum of Modern Art in Aalborg, Denmark and the Hirshhorn Museum in Washington, DC. Her work is in the collections of numerous museums, among them, the Museum of Modern Art, New York; the Metropolitan Museum of Art, New York; the National Portrait Gallery, London; the Whitney Museum of American Art, New York; the Art Institute of Chicago; Harvard Art Museums, Massachusetts; and the Smithsonian National Museum of African Art, Washington, DC. She received her MFA from the California College of the Arts. She lives in New York.

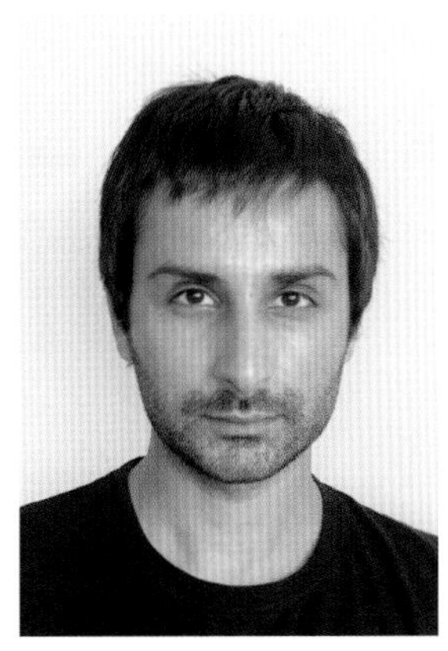

Salman Toor (b. 1983) was born in Lahore, Pakistan. Toor has had two solo museum exhibitions: *No Ordinary Love* at the Baltimore Museum of Art (2022) and *How Will I Know* at the Whitney Museum of American Art (2020–21). Recent exhibitions include *Any Distance between Us* at the RISD Museum in Providence (2021–22) and solo presentations *The Pleasure Pavilion: A Series of Installations* at Luhring Augustine, New York (2020–21), and *I Know a Place* at Nature Morte Gallery, New Delhi, India (2019). His work is in public collections such as the Museum of Contemporary Art Chicago; Tate Modern, London; the RISD Museum, Providence; and the Whitney Museum of American Art, New York. Toor received his MFA from the Pratt Institute. He lives in New York.

Resources

Selected Publications

2022

Chan, T. F. "At Home with Russell Tovey." *Wallpaper**, July 27, 2022.

Simmons, William J. *Queer Formalism: The Return*. Berlin, 2022.

Tompkins, Calvin. "How Salman Toor Left the Old Masters Behind." *The New Yorker*, August 1, 2022.

Truax, Stephen. "Object Lesson: To You." *Manual*, no. 16 (2022). https://publications.risdmuseum.org/issue-16-intimacy/object-lesson-you.

Yerebakan, Osman Can. "7 Artists on the Resilience of Depicting Queer Intimacy in Public." *Artsy*, June 13, 2022.

2021

Kherbek, William. "Ecstatic Communion: *Intimacy* at the Schwules Museum." *Berlin Art Link*, May 25, 2021.

Langberg, Doron, and Salman Toor. "Friends Who Inspire Each Other." *T* Magazine, April 12, 2021.

Lubow, Arthur. "Changing the Perspective." *W* Magazine, November 30, 2021.

Noor, Tausif. "Salman Toor's Cosmopolitan Queer Life." *Frieze*, February 16, 2021.

Urrutia, Cindy, ed. *Nobody Promised You Tomorrow: Art 50 Years after Stonewall*. Exh. cat. Brooklyn (Brooklyn Museum), 2019. Fresno, 2021.

2020

Akel, Joseph. Review of *Intimate Companions*, Provincetown Arts Society, July 3–September 8, 2020. *Artforum*, August 28, 2020. Online.

Campbell, Andy. *Bound Together: Leather, Sex, Archives, and Contemporary Art*. Manchester, 2020.

Diament, Robert, and Russell Tovey. "Salman Toor (NYC Special Episode)." *Talk Art* (podcast), November 12, 2020.

Sokol, Brent. "Can a New Arts Center Revitalize Provincetown?" *New York Times*, July 2, 2020.

2019

Daderko, Dean. *Stonewall 50*. Exh. cat. Houston (Contemporary Arts Museum Houston), 2019.

Earnest, Jarrett, ed. *The Young and Evil: Queer Modernism in New York*. Exh. cat. New York (David Zwirner), 2019.

Lord, Catherine, and Richard Meyer, eds. *Art and Queer Culture*. 2nd rev. ed. New York, 2019.

Malone, Tyler. "Doron Langberg and the New Queer Intimism." *Jewish Currents*, December 9, 2019.

Reed, Christopher, et al. *Art after Stonewall, 1969–1989*. Exh. cat. Columbus (Columbus Museum of Art), 2019.

Schwabsky, Barry. "What's Wrong with the New Figurative Painting?" *The Nation*, October 30, 2019.

2018

Christie-Dervaux, Millie. Review of *Intimacy*, Yossi Milo Gallery, New York, June 28–August 24, 2018. *The Brooklyn Rail*, July/August 2018.

Pham, Larissa. "In Queer Art, There's a Time for Action and a Time for Languor." *Garage*, July 12, 2018.

Small, Zachary. "Looking at Queer Constellations of Intimacy." *Hyperallergic*, August 20, 2018.

Telling, Olly. "Four Artists Busting the Stereotype that Queer Art Has to Be Doom and Gloom." *Dazed*, July 19, 2018.

2017

Small, Zachary. "How Contemporary Artists Are Evolving the Queer Aesthetic." *Artsy*, June 15, 2017.

Truax, Stephen. "Why Young Queer Artists Are Trading Anguish for Joy." *Artsy*, November 7, 2017.

Exhibitions

2022

Living Histories: Queer Views and Old Masters. Curated by Aimee Ng and Xavier F. Salomon. The Frick Collection, New York, September 30, 2021–September 11, 2022.

Queering the Narrative. NAK Neuer Aachener Kunstverein, Aachen, Germany, July 3–August 21, 2022.

Intimacy. Victoria Miro, London, June 8–July 30, 2022.

2021

Any Distance between Us. Curated by Stephen Truax and Dominic Molon. RISD Museum, Providence, July 17, 2021–March 13, 2022.

Equal Affections. Organized in collaboration with Edwin Oostmeijer. Grimm Gallery, Amsterdam, July 23–September 5, 2021.

Breakfast Under the Tree. Curated by Russell Tovey. Carl Freedman Gallery, Margate, June 4–September 4, 2021.

2020

Intimate Companions. Curated by Joe Sheftel. Provincetown Arts Society, July 3–September 8, 2020.

Salman Toor: How Will I Know. Curated by Christopher Y. Lew and Ambika Trasi. Whitney Museum of American Art, New York, November 13, 2020–April 4, 2021.

Intimacy: New Queer Art from Berlin and Beyond. Curated by Peter Rehberg and Apostolos Lampropoulos. Schwules Museum, Berlin, December 3, 2020–August 30, 2021.

2019

The Young and Evil. Curated by Jarrett Earnest. David Zwirner, New York, February 21–April 13, 2019.

Art after Stonewall, 1969–1989. Curated by Jonathan Weinberg with Tyler Cann and Drew Sawyer. Grey Art Gallery and Leslie-Lohman Museum of Gay and Lesbian Art, New York, April 24–July 21, 2019; Patricia and Phillip Frost Art Museum, Miami, September 14, 2019–January 6, 2020; Columbus Museum of Art, March 6–October 4, 2020.

Stonewall 50. Curated by Dean Daderko, based on an exhibition proposed by Bill Arning. Contemporary Arts Museum Houston, April 27–July 28, 2019.

Nobody Promised You Tomorrow: Art 50 Years after Stonewall. Curated by Margo Cohen Ristorucci, Lindsay C. Harris, Carmen Hermo, Allie Rickard, and Lauren Argentina Zelaya. Brooklyn Museum, May 3–December 8, 2019.

Them. Perrotin New York, June 2–August 16, 2019.

2018

Intimacy. Curated by Stephen Truax. Yossi Milo Gallery, New York, June 28–August 24, 2018.

Index

Page numbers in *italics* refer to illustrations.

Image Credits

Photographs have been provided by the owners or custodians of the works.
The following list applies to those photographs for which a separate credit line is due.

Why
Fig. 1: © Doron Langberg / Courtesy the artist and Victoria Miro

"We Can Occupy This Space Now"
Fig. 6: © 2022 Estate of Ad Reinhardt / Artists Rights Society (ARS), NY

Hindsight
Fig. 7: Royal Collection Trust / © His Majesty King Charles III 2022
Fig. 8: Photo John R. Glembin

Catalogue

Jenna Gribbon
Cat. 1: © Jenna Gribbon / Courtesy the artist, The Brant Foundation, and Fredericks & Freiser, NY / Photo Joseph Coscia Jr.
Fig. 9: bpk Bildagentur / Gemäldegalerie, Staatliche Museen zu Berlin / Jörg P. Anders / Art Resource, NY
Figs. 10, 11: Photo Joseph Coscia Jr.
Fig. 13: © Jenna Gribbon / Courtesy MASSIMODECARLO / Photo Adam Reich
Fig. 14: © Jenna Gribbon / Courtesy Fredericks & Freiser, NY

Doron Langberg
Cat. 2: Photo Joseph Coscia Jr.
Figs. 15, 16: Photo Joseph Coscia Jr.
Figs. 18, 20, 21: © Doron Langberg / Courtesy the artist and Victoria Miro
Fig. 19: © The National Gallery, London

Salman Toor
Cat. 3: © Salman Toor / Courtesy the artist and Luhring Augustine, NY / Photo Farzad Owrang
Figs. 22, 24, 26: Photo Joseph Coscia Jr.
Figs. 23, 27, 28: © Salman Toor / Courtesy the artist and Luhring Augustine, NY / Photo Farzad Owrang
Fig. 25: © Christie's Images / Bridgeman Images

Toyin Ojih Odutola
Cat. 4: © Toyin Ojih Odutola / Courtesy the artist and Jack Shainman Gallery, New York
Figs. 29, 30, 31: Photo Joseph Coscia Jr.
Figs. 32–35: © Toyin Ojih Odutola / Courtesy the artist and Jack Shainman Gallery, New York